DELIVERING SERVICES IN
MULTICULTURAL SOCIETIES

NEW FRONTIERS OF SOCIAL POLICY

DELIVERING SERVICES
IN MULTICULTURAL
SOCIETIES

Alexandre Marc

THE WORLD BANK

1818 H Street NW
Washington DC 20433
Telephone: 202-473-1000
Internet: www.worldbank.org
E-mail: feedback@worldbank.org

1 2 3 4 12 11 10 09

This volume is a product of the staff of the International Bank for Reconstruction and Development / The World Bank. The findings, interpretations, and conclusions expressed in this volume do not necessarily reflect the views of the Executive Directors of The World Bank or the governments they represent.

The World Bank does not guarantee the accuracy of the data included in this work. The boundaries, colors, denominations, and other information shown on any map in this work do not imply any judgment on the part of The World Bank concerning the legal status of any territory or the endorsement or acceptance of such boundaries.

ISBN: 978-0-8213-8049-9
eISBN: 978-0-8213-8084-0
DOI: 10.1596/978-0-8213-8049-9

Library of Congress Cataloging-in-Publication Data
Marc, Alexandre, 1956–
    Delivering services in multicultural societies / Alexandre Marc.
        p. cm.
    —(New frontiers of social policy)
    Includes bibliographical references and index.
    ISBN 978-0-8213-8049-9—ISBN 978-0-8213-8084-0 (electronic)
    1. Minorities—Services for. 2. Minorities—Social conditions. 3. Multiculturalism. I. Title.
    HV3176.M36 2009
    362.84— dc22
    2009035883

Cover photo: Tran Thi Hoa, The World Bank
Cover design: Naylor Design

In many developing countries, the mixed record of state effectiveness, market imperfections, and persistent structural inequities has undermined the effectiveness of social policy. To overcome these constraints, social policy needs to move beyond conventional social service approaches toward development's goals of equitable opportunity and social justice. This series has been created to promote debate among the development community, policy makers, and academia, and to broaden understanding of social policy challenges in developing country contexts.

The books in the series are linked to the World Bank's Social Development Strategy. The strategy is aimed at empowering people by transforming institutions to make them more inclusive, responsive, and accountable. This involves the transformation of subjects and beneficiaries into citizens with rights and responsibilities. Themes in this series include equity and development, assets and livelihoods, citizenship and rights-based social policy, and the social dimensions of infrastructure and climate change.

Titles in the series:

- *Assets, Livelihoods, and Social Policy*
- *Building Equality and Opportunity through Social Guarantees: New Approaches to Public Policy and the Realization of Rights*
- *Delivering Services in Multicultural Societies*
- *Inclusive States: Social Policy and Structural Inequalities*
- *Institutional Pathways to Equity: Addressing Inequality Traps*
- *Social Dimensions of Climate Change: Equity and Vulnerability in a Warming World*

Acknowledgments xi
About the Author xiii
Abbreviations xv

Chapter 1: Introduction: Culture and Services 1

Background and Definitions 1
Purpose and Organization 4

Chapter 2: Cultural Diversity and Public Policy 7

Migrations, Minorities, and the Demand for Cultural Recognition 8
A Growing International Recognition of Cultural Rights 12
A New Paradigm: The Concept of Multicultural Citizenship 14
Managing Cultural Diversity through Public Policy 18
Significance of Cultural Diversity in Making Public Policy for
Development and Poverty Reduction 22
The Risks of Taking Culture into Account in Developing Public Policy 26

Chapter 3: Cultural Diversity and Service Delivery 31

Education 31
Health Care 40
Cultural Services 46
Delivering Services through Traditional Local Governance Systems 49

Chapter 4: Designing and Implementing Policies That Support Cultural Diversity in Service Delivery   **57**

A Conceptual Framework to Guide Policies   58
No Universal Solutions   60
Understanding Political Motivations   60
Integrated and Multisectoral Approaches   62
Establishing National Frameworks for Managing Cultural Diversity   64
Establishing Clarity in Decentralization Frameworks   65
Involvement of Concerned Sociocultural Groups   66
Balance between Citizens' Rights and Cultural Rights   67
Socioeconomic Conditions   69
Cost of Multicultural Programs   70
Long-Term Investments and Strategies   71
Evaluation   72

Chapter 5: Adapting Services to a Diverse Society   **75**

Appendix: What Is Cultural Identity?   **79**
Bibliography   **83**
Index   **91**

Boxes

1.1 Definitions   2
2.1 Minority Group Designations and Definitions   10
2.2 UN Recognition of Ethnic and Racial Rights   13
2.3 Agency: A Definition   17
2.4 Dominant Minorities   23
3.1 Success of Multicultural Education Reform in Papua New Guinea   32
3.2 Maori Immersion Education and Education Outcomes   34
3.3 Institutionalized Discrimination: Segregated Schooling for the Roma   36
3.4 Social Inclusion and Preschool in Albania and Kosovo   38
3.5 Considerations in Bilingual Education   40
3.6 Roma Health Mediators in Roma Communities   42

3.7 Traditional Medicines, Contemporary Issues 45
3.8 The Return of the Kanun and the Fis in Albania 51
3.9 Local Governance versus National Citizenship in
    Totontepec, Mexico 54
4.1 The Vicious Cycle of Stereotyping 70
4.2 Lack of Financing Undermines Bulgarian Native Language Policy 71

ACKNOWLEDGMENTS

The author is grateful for the support and advice of Shelton Davis of Georgetown University and for input provided by Abebe Zegeye, Costanza Hermanin, Kelci Lowe, Oscar Augusto Lopez, and Vivian Andreescu. Thanks are also due to Anis Dani, Antonela Capelle-Pogacean, Dena Ringold, Michael Woolcock, Tim Campbell, Caroline Kende-Robb, and Steen Jorgensen for reading and commenting on various drafts; and to Lauri Friedman and Nita Congress for editing the text. This book is an outgrowth of the 2006 World Bank study, "Cultural Diversity and Delivery of Services: A Major Challenge for Social Inclusion."

Alexandre Marc has worked on local development, conflict, and youth inclusion issues around the world, notably in Africa, the Middle East, Latin America, Europe, and East Asia. He is a Lead Social Development Specialist in the World Bank and manages the Conflict, Crime, and Violence team in the Social Development Department. Previously, he was sector manager for Social Development for the Europe and Central Asia Region. In between these two Bank positions, he was Director of the Roma Education Fund, an international foundation based in Budapest that supports the inclusion of Roma children in education systems; and he was a visiting fellow at the Paris Centre d'études et de recherches internationales, where he undertook research on cultural identity and minorities. His publications include "Taking Culture into Account in the Delivery of Health and Education Services," in *Inclusive States: Social Policy and Structural Inequalities* (Anis Dani and Arjan de Haan, eds., World Bank, 2008) and *When Things Fall Apart: Qualitative Studies of Poverty in the Former Soviet Union* (edited with N. Dudwick, E. Gomart, and K. Kuehnast, World Bank, 2003). He holds a doctorate from the Paris Institute of Political Science.

AIDS	acquired immune deficiency syndrome
NGO	nongovernmental organization
OSCE	Organization for Security and Co-operation in Europe
PRI	Partido Revolucionario Institucional (Institutional Revolutionary Party)
UN	United Nations
UNDP	United Nations Development Programme
UNESCO	United Nations Educational, Scientific and Cultural Organization
UNICEF	United Nations Children's Fund
WHO	World Health Organization

CHAPTER 1

Introduction: Culture and Services

The last two decades have witnessed a growing recognition of the importance of taking cultural and ethnic diversity into consideration when designing and implementing development programs. As societies around the world have become more culturally diverse, and the role culture plays in the formation of identity has become better understood, governments are beginning to pay greater attention to the management of cultural diversity and are becoming more sensitive to issues of cultural exclusion. This book explores how taking cultural diversity into account can affect the delivery of services both positively and negatively, and how local governments can respond to the challenge of programming for and around diversity.

Background and Definitions

Cultural diversity—the mingling of groups of different ethnic and religious backgrounds in a society—is becoming increasingly prevalent in countries around the world. According to the 2004 *Human Development Report*, about 5,000 ethnic groups live in nearly 200 countries around the globe; in two-thirds of these countries, one or more ethnic or religious groups account for at least 10 percent of the population (UNDP 2004). This multiculturalism is a product of several globalizing trends, including enhanced mobility. Alongside this increasing diversity is a growing need on the part of many groups to assert or reassert their identity in a rapidly homogenizing world. Bringing these factors into alignment with the move toward a global society understandably creates a major challenge for national governments, local governments, and the providers of public services charged with designing social policies and ensuring social cohesion and integration.

(See box 1.1 for definitions of these and other terms used in this book; see the appendix for a discussion of the concept of cultural identity.)

Cultural diversity has of course always existed, but three broad phenomena underlie and define cultural diversity as experienced in today's world.

- *Mobility.* The rate of contemporary migrations,[1] both international and national, has created many mixed communities of differing origins and cultures living in the same territory and under the same local administration. However, unlike earlier generations of immigrants, today's migrants can maintain much stronger ties to their country or

---

BOX 1.1

Definitions

- *Culture* refers to the values, norms, and institutions that regulate social life and the interactions among members of a society that shape their collective vision of the world. A culture evolves and constantly adjusts to internal and external influences. As noted social anthropologist Mary Douglas wrote: "In reality, the connected meanings that are the basis of any given culture are multiplex, precarious, complex and fluid. They are continually contested and always in the process of mutual accommodation. The dialogue leads to a concentration of meanings. It is the process of self-understanding, the way the community explains itself to itself and others" (Douglas 2004, p. 88).
- *Hybridization* is the process by which a culture adopts aspects of other cultures. This process occurs on a smaller scale when individuals of one culture assimilate traits of another.
- *Social cohesion* refers to the way a group, community, or society reacts collectively to internal or external challenges. A cohesive society—which does not have to be culturally homogenous—minimizes internal conflict, and its members collaborate effectively to resolve problems or combat external threats.
- *Social integration* refers to the ability of individuals or groups to participate economically, socially, and politically in a broader community or society. It assumes that members of the group or society share at least some of the same values and vision.
- *Social inclusion* also refers to the ability of individuals or groups to be part of a broader community, but it places less emphasis on shared values and vision, and focuses instead on access to basic rights and functions.

community of origin, in large part because of technologies that have made it easier and less expensive to communicate with those left behind. This ease of connection to their native culture reinforces migrants' sense of belonging to that culture and somewhat mitigates the desire to integrate fully into the new community.

• *Demand for recognition of cultural identity.* Around the world, ethnocultural minorities are demanding greater recognition and accommodation of their cultural practices and identities. Migrants and members of minority groups are today less likely to adopt automatically the dominant culture and to discard their own cultural practices or keep them private. Nations and societies are responding to this shift. In this regard, political philosopher Will Kymlicka notes:

> In the last forty years, we have witnessed a veritable revolution around the world in the relations between states and ethnocultural minorities. Older models of assimilationist and homogenizing nation-states are increasingly being contested, and often displaced, by newer multicultural models of the state and citizenship. This is reflected, for example, in the widespread adoption of cultural and religious accommodations for immigrant groups, the acceptance of territorial autonomy and language rights for national minorities, and the recognition of land claims and self-government rights for indigenous peoples (Kymlicka 2007, p. 3).

• *Changes in models of self-identification.* Traditional bases of identity, such as profession and family, are changing dramatically and consequently losing some of their social, cultural, and emotional appeal (Dubar 2000). Labor markets are becoming more fluid and flexible, with people changing jobs and careers more frequently. Families are being transformed as marriage becomes less important to social recognition. In explaining these trends, which are primarily seen in the developed world but are also evident among the middle classes of the developing world as well, French sociologist Alain Touraine (2005) develops the idea that the last two centuries were "social," in the sense that human beings thought of themselves as members of society and subscribed to the concept of citizenship. Today, people tend to reject the idea of self-determination by social structure and an identity defined by a social model. Contemporary identities are more narrative, with people defining themselves by their personal story and culture. This phenomenon has a major impact on identity formation and social organization. It also poses a severe challenge to social cohesion and inclusion, as individuals cannot and do not rely on family and professional networks as they once did for support and direction.

Purpose and Organization

Much social scientific research has been conducted on issues and policies that deal with economic and political integration at the national level; this research has addressed the political and institutional mechanisms that are set up to ensure that various groups can live together cohesively and share resources equitably. Numerous studies have addressed, for instance, the integration of African-American communities in the United States; the problem of recognizing new rights for the indigenous communities of Canada; and the challenge of integrating new migrant populations in England, France, and Germany. Until recently, the idea of looking at *cultural* as well as economic and political inclusion has received relatively little attention from either academics or public policy makers. A further shortcoming in the attempt to understand and address cultural diversity is the fact that studies have focused on the national level, whereas evidence shows that much of the demand for recognition of cultural identity occurs at the *local* level, specifically, in municipalities and local communities. Information at this level is scarce, particularly in terms of helping to formulate a community response to this demand while delivering basic services.

This book looks at ways in which culture influences access to services and attempts to show some possible directions to follow in making the delivery of services more sensitive to cultural diversity. A lack of source material prevents an exhaustive treatment of the topic of cultural diversity in service delivery, but it does permit the identification of key trends and issues.

The following chapter presents the current debate on the role of governments—at all levels—in managing cultural diversity. It examines why cultural diversity is recognized as a legitimate field for policy making and demonstrates the increased international interest in recognizing minority and cultural rights. It also identifies the risks and benefits of accepting cultural diversity as an issue for social policy and presents the context for current policies that deal with cultural diversity.

Chapter 3 takes a more in-depth look at specific areas in which the demand for recognition of cultural practices in the delivery of services is strongest:

- *Education*, mostly related to the issue of instruction in native languages
- *Health care*, including the recognition of specific medicinal practices
- *Cultural services*, such as the provision and promotion of cultural centers, religious and national festivals, and traditional forms of cultural expression

The chapter then looks at the role of traditional local governance in service delivery and the implications of that role for policy development.

Chapter 4 examines policies pertaining to basic service delivery that can address and support cultural diversity. Developing such policies is challenging for two reasons:

- Impact analysis of policies and programs that support cultural diversity remains limited.
- Diversity is a relatively new focus for governments and international organizations.

Actions that support cultural diversity must be integrated into general social and economic policies in order to be effective. The answer is not to develop parallel policies, but to make cultural diversity a mainstream priority for government policies and programs.

Chapter 5 summarizes the lessons learned from the design of culturally sensitive policies for delivering services to a diverse population. Improved inclusion will, in most cases, require policies that support recognition of minority groups' cultural specificity and that can directly improve their socioeconomic status. Failure to recognize the connection between culture and economy can push groups into further exclusion and poverty even while supporting their demand for cultural recognition.

Note

1. According to the United Nations Department of Economic and Social Affairs (2009), the number of international migrants in 2005 was estimated to be 195 million, or 3 percent of the world's population that year; these figures would be even higher taking national migrations—those that occur within a country's borders—into account.

CHAPTER 2

Cultural Diversity and Public Policy

Today, about 190 independent states are home to about 5,000 ethnic groups and 600 living languages; two-thirds of the states have at least one ethnic or religious minority that makes up at least 10 percent of the population (UNDP 2004). These groups are increasingly mobilizing along religious, ethnic, and cultural lines, demanding that their particularities be recognized by broader society. In Latin America, grievances over an increasingly unequal society tend to be based in ethnic divisions. In the Arab world, religion has replaced the secular and socialist Arab nationalism of the 1960s as the major political force. In parts of Asia, the push toward ethno-cultural self-identification is resulting in rising ethnic and religious violence and conflict. Migrants around the world are increasingly rejecting the notion that their culture of origin should be a private matter and are resisting majority society pressure to publicly adopt the dominant culture. Minority cultures are fighting not only for increased political participation but also for official recognition of their languages, religions, and festivals. As a result, governments across the world are increasingly engaged in finding ways to manage the diverse societies and groups that form part of the countries they govern. Nondemocratic countries tend to rely on repressive approaches; but in more open societies, managing cultural diversity is becoming a focus of public policy, and policies aimed at social inclusion and social cohesion are becoming more pervasive.

This chapter first reviews how the migration and movement of populations have contributed to an increased recognition on the part of governments worldwide of the need for better public policies to manage cultural diversity. It then reviews the progress toward an international framework on the issue of cultural rights, and looks at how the concept of multicultural citizenship is taking root in many countries. Finally, the chapter looks at how public policy aims to manage cultural diversity and to address this diversity in achieving overarching societal goals.

Migrations, Minorities, and the Demand for Cultural Recognition

According to the United Nations, the number of international migrants grew from 75 million in 1965 to 150 million in 1990. In 2005, there were 195 million international migrants, and the average annual increase in their number was greater than overall world population growth itself (United Nations Department of Economic and Social Affairs 2009). Many of these migrants moved from developing to developed countries, but migration from poor developing countries to developing middle-income countries is also on the rise. In 2005, two out of every five migrants resided in a developing country (Ratha and Shaw 2007). The Gulf countries have always received large numbers of migrants from other Arab countries as well as from Asia. Argentina has absorbed sizable flows of migrants from Bolivia, Paraguay, and Peru. The República Bolivariana de Venezuela has long been a migration destination for Colombians and Ecuadorians. There are about a million illegal workers from Indonesia in Malaysia. More than 1 million Mozambicans are in South Africa, a country whose mining sector, which has always used migrant workers from neighboring countries, is now estimated to be 300,000 persons strong. In the mid-1990s, one-quarter of the population in the Côte d'Ivoire came from Burkina Faso, Mali, Niger, and other neighboring countries from the north. Africa's many political crises and civil wars have prompted refugees to move across borders.

Migration between high-income countries is also increasing, reflecting the trend toward a global labor market. Rapid progress in technology sectors, as well as the opening of new economic opportunities in places such as the European Union, further facilitate the movement of human resources.

Migration is generally associated with the crossing of *national* borders; however, internal migrations account for large numbers of migrants, and such movements are increasing. Close to 140 million people were estimated to have migrated internally in China in 2008, compared to about 500,000 international migrants from China the same year (Sheineson 2009).

Rural-to-rural migrations continue to be significant in developing countries. In India, rural migration accounted for roughly 62 percent of all movements in 1999–2000. These migrants are mostly rural poor looking for work as laborers in richer agricultural areas. Similar migrations take place in Senegal around groundnut cultivation. Rural-to-urban migration is also on the rise in many countries. Interestingly, urban-to-rural migrations are not rare either. Many Chinese migrants go back to their village of origin after working in urban centers for some time (Ping and Shahau 2005). Urban-to-rural migration also occurs during economic crises or political upheavals. In countries of the former Soviet Union, many workers returned to rural areas to survive the economic collapse that followed the union's dissolution.

Urban-to-urban migration is the predominant form of migration in Latin America. In Mexico, half of the interstate migrations made between 1987 and 1992 were between urban areas; this percentage had increased to 70 percent between 1995 and 2000 (Deshingar and Grimm 2005). Most urban-to-urban migrations involved a move from a smaller center to a larger center. In Albania, for instance, the strategy adopted by most migrants is to move from villages, especially in the north, to the capital city of Tirana in incremental steps. They move first to a small regional center, then to a bigger one, then to Tirana, and then eventually abroad.

Such migrations are in large part attributable to inequalities among regions and countries. Such inequalities are not only income based, but also opportunity based—that is, the result of inequitable access to basic services and security. They also reflect inequalities in freedom of choice (Sen 1999). The greater autonomy available to individuals in Western economies or even in developing country urban centers is very attractive, especially to youth. The pressure to conform to ancestral collective norms and habits is often cited by young migrants in developing countries as a reason to move to urban centers or abroad.[1]

The exponential increase in population movement throughout the world makes for constant confrontations of different lifestyles and values, since many of these migrations involve people of one culture settling in a community with a majority population of another culture. The impact of migration on the awareness of cultural differences is strong. Very little quantitative data are available on the impact of migration on ethnic identity and culture, but many qualitative assessments reveal this to be an important issue for individuals' well-being (Brettell 2003; Benmayor and Skotnes 2005). For instance, indigenous populations (see box 2.1 for definitions of terms related to minority populations) comprise many of the rural-to-urban migrants in Bolivia, Ecuador, Guatemala, and Peru; these people are moving to urban centers populated by a Hispanic majority. Many migrants to Côte d'Ivoire are poor Muslims from the Sahelian cultural area to the

BOX 2.1

Minority Group Designations and Definitions

- An *ethnic group* is one that self-identifies or is recognized by others (the majority) as different because of its historical or biological particularities. An ethnic minority might or might not share customs and values with the majority population, but its differences often result in a split from the main population and can create strong differences in identity.
- A *cultural minority* is a group that self-identifies or is recognized by others as having different values, customs, and social practices from the main population. It can be differentiated ethnically, religiously, or linguistically or in terms of certain preferences and practices that diverge from those of the main population.
- *Indigenous peoples* are those that have inhabited a territory longer than other groups in the general population (which have, in most cases, colonized the indigenous population's territories) and that have strong economic, social, and spiritual collective connections with this territory which are embedded in their customs, beliefs, and local institutions. Indigenous people are dependent on these connections for their survival as a particular group and are thus often vulnerable to rapid external changes.
- A *national minority* is a group that differs from the majority population by virtue of its symbolic and historic connection to a territory and a collective shared history. It usually shares a specific symbolic identity (such as a flag, national anthem, or set of recognized holidays).

north moving into southern forest lands largely populated by animist and Christian populations. In China, tensions and cultural clashes commonly result from migrations of the dominant Han population into Tibet and Xinjiang. In France, Islam has become the second largest religion in the country after Catholicism, a change that has created its own set of tensions.

Migrants are increasingly less inclined to renounce their cultural norms and values when moving abroad. Although drawn to a particular country because it offers opportunities or security, they feel little need to give up their native culture in exchange for these benefits. Trying to maintain one's cultural identity when moving across boundaries is not a new endeavor, but it has become more legitimate of late. Numerous authors, anthropologists, and sociologists argue that today, as part of the globalization process, the link between territory and culture has weakened, in that people retain their own culture and its particular way of life, values, and beliefs even when living among others, making less of an attempt to integrate into the larger society (Tomlinson 1999). The massive unilateral flows of migration of the 18th and 19th centuries—such as the Irish emigration to the United States in the wake of the potato blight or the move of the Basques, Galicians, and Italians to Argentina—were experienced as a major economic, social, and cultural uprooting and a clear break with the community of origin. This is no longer the case. Modern migration is often temporary or, when longer term, accompanied by many back-and-forth moves to and from the region of origin. Over the last 50 years, technological progress, along with more affordable transportation and communication developments, has kept migrants better connected to their communities of origin. This technological revolution has had an enormous impact on the identity of migrant communities.

The failure of the majority system to adequately reward adoption of the dominant culture, either economically or socially, has also played into migrants' reluctance to give up their culture. It is clear that becoming culturally French, British, or German, for example, does not guarantee economic equity. Australia, Canada, and the United States are among the few countries where becoming part of the mainstream culture is believed to bring economic benefits, and where, to some extent, it does. (This is generally true of countries in which people of migrant origin make up the majority of the population.) Migrants also tend to hold fast to their native culture when confronted with a disconnect between their own values and those of the culture of the host country, especially regarding issues related to gender and family.

Demand for recognition of cultural specificity and diverse cultural identity comes not only from migrant populations: it also comes from minority groups that have been part of particular nations for many generations, but now believe their values and culture are facing specific threats. This too is not a recent phenomenon, but it has increased with globalization. Today, even the most remote communities have contact with other cultures via radio, television, film, the Internet, the telephone, new goods and services, or simply stories imparted by members of the community who have migrated. Such contact can increase a group's fear of being swallowed up by and lost in a majority or global culture.

Subcultures within a society may also seek recognition of their identity. Youth subculture is a relatively familiar phenomenon in this regard.

Subcultures tend to be local, related to some specific territory (such as a ghetto), but they can also cut across geographic boundaries, creating global cultural connections through fashion, music, and dance (for example, rap, hip hop, or—among North African youth—rai). These subcultures often create connections among various ethnic groups. The French film *La Haine* by Mathieu Kassovitz, which tells the story of three young people searching for meaning in their lives after violent uprisings in poor suburban Parisian neighborhoods, illustrates how subcultures are created across ethnic boundaries. In this case a Jew, an Arab, and a Sub-Saharan African find commonality in their sense of isolation from mainstream French people. Additionally, subcultures are increasingly being built around sexual preference. This is a phenomenon mostly of rich industrialized countries, but is also occurring in the urban centers of developing countries. Members of these communities are asking to be accepted not only for their behaviors, but also for a certain subculture they have created; gay pride parades are a good example of this phenomenon.

A Growing International Recognition of Cultural Rights

In 1966, the United Nations (UN) adopted two important international treaties based on the 1948 Universal Declaration of Human Rights: the International Covenant on Economic, Social and Cultural Rights and the International Covenant on Civil and Political Rights. A new era of international recognition of the rights of persons belonging to ethnic, religious, linguistic, and other minorities was thereby ushered in,[2] and a series of further declarations and conventions were crafted by way of systematically including issues relating to the cultural and other rights of these peoples in the international human rights agenda (box 2.2).

In November 2001, at the 31st session of the United Nations Educational, Scientific and Cultural Organization (UNESCO) General Conference, the representatives of participating governments unanimously approved the Universal Declaration on Cultural Diversity. The first of the declaration's 12 articles characterizes the world's rich cultural diversity as a common heritage of humanity that "should be recognized and affirmed for the benefit of present and future generations" and notes that "as a source of exchange, innovation and creativity, cultural diversity is as necessary for humankind as biodiversity is for nature" (UNESCO 2002). The UNESCO declaration highlights the important role cultural diversity can and should

BOX 2.2

UN Recognition of Ethnic and Racial Rights

Since 1966, the United Nations and a number of its specialized agencies have taken definitive action to promote more favorable treatment of ethnic minorities and racial groups.

- In 1978, the United Nations Educational, Scientific, and Cultural Organization (UNESCO) issued a special Declaration on Race and Racial Prejudice, as follow-up to the 1965 International Convention on the Elimination of All Forms of Racial Discrimination.
- In 1989, the International Labour Organization approved Convention 169, Concerning Indigenous and Tribal Peoples in Independent Countries.
- In 1992, the UN General Assembly adopted Resolution 47:135, which became the first international Declaration on the Rights of Persons Belonging to National or Ethnic, Religious or Linguistic Minorities. Article 1 calls upon states to "protect the existence and the national or ethnic, cultural, religious and linguistic identity of minorities within their respective territories and encourage conditions for the promotion of that identity." Article 4 establishes that states shall take measures to "ensure that persons belonging to minorities may exercise fully and effectively all their human rights and fundamental freedoms without any discrimination and in full equality before the law" and "create favourable conditions to enable persons belonging to minorities to express their characteristics and to develop their culture, language, religion, traditions, and customs."
- In 1988, UNESCO launched the World Decade for Cultural Development, which aimed to foster greater international awareness of the critical role recognition of living cultural heritages and more positive cultural policies could play in development.

play in informing government social inclusion, civil society participation, and development policies. Articles 4 through 6 underscore the relationship between human rights and cultural diversity, especially in terms of the "rights of persons belonging to minorities and those of indigenous peoples," focusing on the role of cultural rights as an enabling environment for cultural diversity. In 2004, the United Nations Development Programme took on the topic of cultural liberty as the theme of its annual *Human Development Report*, reviewing policies dealing with cultural diversity and making recommendations on how countries could establish strong participation and recognition of minority cultures.

Concurrent with these UN initiatives, the European Union also looked to address the issue of cultural diversity and minority rights. Through the Organization of Security and Cooperation in Europe and its predecessor agency, the Commission on Security and Cooperation in Europe, the earliest specific principles on minority rights in European space were established. The broadest spectrum of minority rights is provided by the 1990 Document of the Copenhagen Meeting of the Conference on the Human Dimension of the Commission on Security and Cooperation in Europe and was followed up by the creation of the Office of the High Commissioner on National Minorities in 1992. Additionally, the Council of Europe has produced two treaties dealing with issues of minorities and cultural recognition: the Charter on Regional or Minority Languages of 1992 and the Framework Convention for the Protection of National Minorities in 1995. Although the former does not establish individual or collective rights for the speakers, it was established to protect and promote languages. The council claims it is the first multicultural treaty of its kind.[3] These treaties and principles have become benchmarks for accessing the European Union and have contributed to noteworthy legislative changes in the region.

Despite this progress in establishing an international framework for the recognition and management of cultural diversity, ratification of these treaties by national governments has been slow, and their application in countries even more so. This being said, some countries have made timely progress in this area. New Zealand, for instance, has made substantial and impressive efforts toward including its Maori population while simultaneously recognizing its individuality. Canada has found ways to accommodate its various cultures into a multicultural nation, successfully surmounting the constitutional crisis of the 1970s. And countries with contexts as diverse as Colombia, Ecuador, Hungary, and Malaysia have put the recognition of cultural diversity at the forefront of their legislative and constitutional reform agendas. Overall, however, much work remains to be done, and major discrepancies exist between national legislations and the frameworks established by international organizations.

A New Paradigm: The Concept of Multicultural Citizenship

Because very few countries are ethnically homogeneous (only Iceland, the Democratic People's Republic of Korea, and the Republic of Korea are considered such), the question of how a government should manage cultural diversity is not new. States have dealt with clashes over languages, political participation, land claims, local autonomy, and access to services by various ethnic or cultural groups for millennia. With the rise of nation-states in the 19th and 20th centuries, however, governments' dominant approach shifted toward trying to build a unique citizenship that would become the prime identity of the inhabitants of the given country. It was believed that various ethnic and cultural identities, along with their specific histories, languages, customs, and beliefs, would disappear over time or be totally confined to the private realm. Modernity was seen as an integrating force that would accelerate this process, rendering various practices and beliefs obsolete as they hindered both the improvement of living standards and efforts to evolve into a technocratic society (Giddens 1990). From the French Revolution, with its centralized emphasis and violent imposition of a revolutionary citizenship, through the various totalitarian models of the 20th century and "comrade citizenship" of the Soviet Union, a vision of unity and integration was promulgated.

After World War II and the concomitant demonstration of the extreme to which the concept of a nation's ethnic purity could be pushed, the model of a unique culture that supplants or excludes all others began to be contested. Democracies realized that cultural diversity needed to be recognized, but many liberals thought that defining universal human rights would adequately deal with this issue. Rather than protecting vulnerable cultural groups directly (by granting special rights for them), cultural minorities would be protected indirectly by guaranteeing basic civil and political rights to all individuals regardless of group membership (Kymlicka 1995). Guided by this philosophy, the United Nations deleted all references to the rights of ethnic and national minorities in its 1948 Universal Declaration of Human Rights. Countries were nonetheless left to deal pragmatically with cultural diversity. In Europe, Belgium, Spain, and Switzerland are among the countries that have instituted political arrangements that clearly recognize the cultural diversity of their citizenry.

Minority rights have since returned to prominence, and today's policy makers and academics believe that, to avoid conflicts and support social cohesion and inclusion, governments need to supplement traditional human rights with minority and cultural ones (Kymlicka 2007). The French political scientist Michel Wieviorka (1993) presents four models of social inclusion for culturally diverse democracies: the communitarian approach, the assimilationist approach, the integrationist approach, and the multiculturalist approach.

- *The communitarian approach.* This approach focuses on the importance of considering the culture of various social groups. It does not require the different groups to adopt a national culture, but rather establishes a legal and institutional framework that allows these various communities to keep their values, institutions, habits, and way of life while living in the state. For example, a communitarian organization would employ separate legal and judicial systems for different groups (as in Israel, where Arab Israelis and Jewish Israelis each have their own separate legal and judicial systems) or offer different forms of local government (as in some indigenous communities in Colombia). In some cases, separate education systems might be established. This approach is often criticized for keeping communities "inward looking" and for failing to create a common development dynamic.

- *The assimilationist approach.* This approach promotes just one culture in the public sphere. It can be a new culture created to integrate all other cultural groups, as in the republican and secular concept of citizenship best illustrated by the French model which was established during the 1789 revolution. It promotes a single official language for national communication and interaction. Proactive policies encourage all members of society to adopt the dominant culture and drop their other identities. This approach claims that adopting a unique culture guarantees all members of society true equity, while recognizing other cultures undermines social cohesion and creates bias.

- *The integrationist approach.* The goal of this approach is to encourage different cultural groups to live harmoniously under a unique public system. This system respects various cultural and social identities so long as they strive for integration in one broad culture in public life and keep their other identities private. In other words, a singular culture and national identity prevail, but others are tolerated as long as they do not undermine social cohesion. This is the model employed in the United States. As employed there, the model strongly emphasizes patriotism and public recognition of the original values of American society, but tolerates the existence and expression of other identities and cultures in the private realm.

- *The multiculturalist approach.* This approach stresses that maintaining and practicing one's culture is important for identity and agency (box 2.3). It recognizes that people tend to contest a unilateral model of integration, and also that they might want to belong to two or more cultures simultaneously. The model does not support a return to the idea

BOX 2.3

Agency: A Definition

Human agency is the capacity to make choices and to impose those choices on the world. Agency is not a purely utilitarian notion about the ability to change one's material situation. Rather, it is much broader, encompassing the satisfaction of being what one wishes to be. This sense of achievement increases the well-being of the individual, even if it might not have an immediate impact on one's ability to act and increase one's revenue. Economist Amartya Sen (1999) argues that freedom and choice have a value in and of themselves, independent of the effect they have on one's material condition; he sees culture and values as fundamental to agency.

that the state should be comprised of various communities that have no interaction with each other. Rather, it supports a system built around a concept of citizenship based on universal rights shared by all members of society. It encourages some commonly shared core values and a sense of connectivity among all people, but recognizes specific minority and cultural rights. The multiculturalist model is, in practice, one toward which many democracies are starting to move, even if the political discourse continues to be, in many cases, integrationist.

Kymlicka has developed a theory of multicultural citizenship that is winning wide acceptance among contemporary academics and policy makers. In *Multicultural Citizenship*, he writes:

> I believe it is legitimate, and indeed unavoidable, to supplement traditional human rights with minority rights. A comprehensive theory of justice in a multicultural state will include both universal rights, assigned to individuals regardless of group membership, and certain group-differentiated rights or "special status" for minority culture (Kymlicka 1995, p. 6).

Multicultural citizenship preserves a central core of common human rights that are extended to all citizens, but complements these rights with specific ones for minority groups. These specific cultural rights ostensibly allow minorities to exercise their universal rights because they will thus be less discriminated against. "A liberal view requires freedom within the minority group, and equality between the minority and majority groups," Kymlicka (1995, p. 152) notes, and this is what multicultural citizenship aims to achieve.

Managing Cultural Diversity through Public Policy

Many countries have dealt with managing diversity for centuries—Spain has tried to find a balance between various regions, Switzerland has attempted to manage three linguistic groups, and the United States has struggled to integrate its African-American minority. Despite these efforts, viewing the management of diverse cultures as a legitimate public policy concern is a relatively new conception. For a long time, states have resisted such an approach, seeing efforts to legitimize cultural diversity as a direct attack on the integrity of the nation-state and the concept of citizenship. With a few notable exceptions, it is only in the last 20 years that these ideas about and efforts at managing cultural diversity have been developed into policies.

Policies recognizing the specific cultural rights of a particular group are usually justified on the basis of a perceived perception of inequity between sociocultural groups in accessing resources/services and/or in their respective political participation. Usually this inequality results from discrimination or unfairly shared resources and assets owing to a variety of historical, regional, or other reasons. In this context, the rights involved are not cultural, but universal—that is, of an economic, social, or political nature.

The issue of cultural rights—having the freedom to express one's culture—is a separate consideration, but one which is increasingly being regarded as having as much legitimacy as universal rights. The 2004 *Human Development Report* directly links the management of cultural diversity with the recognition of cultural rights:

> Cultural liberty is a vital part of human development because being able to choose one's identity, who one is, without losing the respect of others or being excluded from other choices is important in leading a full life. People want the freedom to practice their religion openly, to speak their language, to celebrate their ethnic or religious heritage without fear of ridicule or punishment or diminished opportunity. People want the freedom to participate in society without having to slip off their chosen cultural mooring (UNDP 2004, p. 1).

To ensure these universal and cultural rights, public policies supporting cultural diversity usually have the following objectives:

- Supporting political participation
- Fighting discrimination
- Reducing cultural exclusion

Supporting Political Participation

Political participation policies usually aim at ensuring the political participation of different groups. Much literature exists on this topic. Ghai (1998) classifies these policies into two main categories: spatial devolution and corporate decentralization. Spatial devolution policies are applied when cultural differences correspond to a territory, while policies relying on corporate decentralization and some form of cultural autonomy are used to provide a framework for the political participation of a minority group independent of the territory in which they live. Such decentralization can take the form of federalism, as when a given territorial community within a central state is granted special status or autonomy. In developing countries, federal states were created at the time of decolonization, and were seen by the colonial power as a way to ensure some form of cohesion in multiethnic states:

> On the whole, colonially devised or inspired federations were not distinguished by their longevity (Indonesia, Burma [Myanmar], Eritrea-Ethiopia, East and West Pakistan, Ghana, Kenya, Uganda). They were introduced at the terminal stages of decolonization, superimposed on centralized and bureaucratic systems, and it proved easy to claw back, de jure or de facto, regional powers (Ghai 1998, p. 43).

However, there have been more successful cases, such as India, Malaysia, Nigeria, and Papua New Guinea. These various arrangements have given rise to a variety of systems that ensure political representation at the national and state levels.

Decentralizing to smaller units of government without establishing autonomous regions is often seen as the best way to ensure participation of various groups. The decentralization approach complements a general trend that encourages devolution of responsibilities to lower levels of governments independently of the issue of cultural diversity. This devolution is usually accomplished to increase citizens' involvement in their own decisions, and to improve the quality of service by bringing the provider closer to the client. This trend is supported by international organizations, which have encouraged states to provide a greater voice to various minorities in the management of their territories. In Latin America, for example, many countries have recently modified their constitution to provide some degree of territorial autonomy to their indigenous population. The constitutional reforms in Colombia in 1991, in Bolivia in 1995, in Ecuador in 1998, and in the República Bolivariana de Venezuela in 2000 all clearly provide rights to indigenous populations in managing the territories in which they live.

Corporate devolution consists of providing special representation to some groups independent of their territorial affiliation. These policies usually consist of reserving special seats in parliaments for groups that tend to be excluded in the normal political process. In this way, the recognized tribes and castes in India, for instance, have seats reserved for them in the parliament. Some groups are also charged with the responsibility of managing their communities, especially in the area of justice. Israel, for example, has separate judicial systems for Jews and for Arab Israelis. Similarly, in Egypt, Christians have different common laws than do Muslims. Consultation mechanisms on policies also involve representatives of minorities or religious institutions.

Fighting Discrimination

Policies that deal with cultural diversity usually seek to ensure some form of equity between groups. As such, their goal is to fight both overt and hidden discrimination. These policies have social inclusion as their objective and, to some extent, social cohesion as well. The 2004 *Human Development Report* (UNDP 2004) distinguishes three different subpolicies:

- Addressing unequal social investments to achieve equality of opportunity
- Recognizing claims to land and livelihoods
- Implementing affirmative actions in favor of disadvantaged groups

Addressing unequal social investment is usually not very different from poverty targeting (discussed later in this chapter), as this is an issue in regions where minorities are overrepresented among the poor and this action might be taken independently of any recognition of a specific culture. However, in some cases, ensuring equal benefit of social investments will also require recognizing some specific cultural rights. For example, certain sanitation regulations might go against particular religious beliefs, therefore depriving minorities of the benefit of this infrastructure. The preparation of kosher food for Jews, for example, might require changing laws that pertain to slaughterhouses.

Minorities have often been excluded from land ownership for historical reasons. Policies addressing this problem have two components. One is linked to land reform, by which unequal distribution of land is addressed through reform of land ownership. The other component involves recognizing collective land claims, mostly submitted by indigenous communities, and returning land to them under their collective management. This latter course of action is not without conflict, especially when these lands are the site of valuable national resources, such as oil. Returning land to collective ownership will, in many cases, also require specific legislation.

Affirmative action attempts to counteract discrimination that is based on negative stereotypes—a complex endeavor, particularly in societies where the sociocultural groups rarely interact, thus leading to self-confirming stereotypes. In this regard, Loury (2001) has used economic reasoning to deconstruct the process by which African Americans are discriminated against in the United States. He clarifies the differences between stereotypes, stigma, and actual discrimination. *Stereotyping* is the way in which people use what they have heard, read, or experienced about a certain group of people to judge and identify the potential behavior of a specific person from that group. People do "a statistical generalization," in Loury's words; this generalization can have a negative, neutral, or positive impact. In a world of limited information, everyone uses stereotypes to some degree. *Stigma* exists when a negative stereotype is systematized so that people are unable to escape being negatively assessed by others. Stigma can also exist for purely cultural reasons, with no specific stereotypes attached. For example, if a person is from a lower caste in India, they are directly stigmatized. *Discrimination* is when this stigma is acted upon, depriving a person or group of the same opportunity or treatment enjoyed by the rest of the population.

Stereotypes are built over time and passed from generation to generation. They are difficult to modify, and, because they are often embedded in culture and attitudes, tend to be very powerful. In addition, many stereotypes tend to be self-confirming, in the sense that the group being stereotyped will anticipate these and act accordingly. This behavior then confirms to outsiders that the stereotype is true.[4] Discrimination based on stigma is very difficult to deal with and usually does not disappear until affirmative action policies can ensure that people are able to exercise their rights and change stereotypes.

Affirmative action allocates access to services, assets, housing, and political participation on the basis of membership in a disadvantaged group. The legacy of affirmative action is a contested one. Affirmative action has successfully reduced intergroup inequalities in places where it has been effectively implemented, but a number of studies have shown it has not reduced inequalities among individuals. Nonetheless, in a country where there are very strong stigmas associated with some groups, affirmative action might be the only way to change stereotypes and reduce informal discrimination. India, for instance, has implemented very active antidiscrimination policies in line with Gandhi's vision of a more tolerant and open society. These policies have resulted in tremendous changes to the nature of India's middle class and its political processes. Even if everyday discrimination still exists against lower castes and tribes, their participation in the administration and in politics has changed Indian society.[5]

Reducing Cultural Exclusion

This area of policy is most directly linked to cultural rights. A person's behavior and way of life are influenced by his or her culture. In a multicultural democracy, living this culture is a right as long as it does not infringe on others' individual rights or on members of the concerned group.

Social exclusion based on one's culture can deprive individuals of the satisfaction of asserting their identity, which is in itself an issue. Moreover, such exclusion can prevent people from accessing services, employment, or justice. For instance, if a Bolivian Quechua Indian is barred from a municipal building because he is wearing a traditional outfit, he is thereby deprived of his basic right to access services. Similarly, nomads are prevented from participating in the political process if they are required to have a fixed home and mailing address in order to cast a vote. This premise can be extended to areas such as respecting customary laws or freedom of religious affiliation.

Examples of policies that fight cultural exclusion include allowing nomadic populations to have an address in a municipality without actually residing in that municipality; allowing certain groups to use customary law to resolve small offenses, so they do not spend time and money trying to access the formal justice system; and allowing people to practice certain livelihoods that might be forbidden to the community at large (such as hunting on reservations), because it is closely associated with their livelihood.

An overriding concern of policies addressing cultural exclusion is to ensure that an individual's choices are respected, and that no one is forced to participate in cultural practices. The groups should have, for instance, the freedom to adopt or abandon their religion, to practice or ignore festivals and various rituals, to teach or be taught languages, and so on. Ensuring this autonomy and individual freedom can be problematic and must be approached thoughtfully.

Significance of Cultural Diversity in Making Public Policy for Development and Poverty Reduction

The literature on culture and cultural diversity cites several reasons recognizing cultural identity is important. This section focuses on three of the main arguments: its role in poverty targeting, its positive impact on agency, and its ability to reduce the risk of conflict.

Poverty Targeting

Cultural minorities are often among the poorest in a given society (but not always, as discussed in box 2.4). Notably, the 8 million Roma in Central Europe are significantly represented among the poorest peoples of the region. A recent survey found that nearly 80 percent of Roma in Romania and Bulgaria were living on less than $4.30 per day. Even in Hungary, one of the most prosperous accession countries, 40 percent of Roma live below the poverty line (Ringold, Orenstein, and Williams 2003). To improve the well-being of such minorities, their cultural specificity must be recognized and antipoverty programs tailored to their needs and culture designed.

A recent study by the World Bank on indigenous populations (Hall and Patrinos 2009) estimates that of a total of about 300 million indigenous people and recognized ethnic minorities around the world, 100 million are considered poor in terms of being under the national poverty line. The study finds that indigenous and ethnic minorities are poorer than the average population in all the countries assessed and that the poverty gap between indigenous and nonindigenous populations has increased over the

---

BOX 2.4

Dominant Minorities

There are well-known cases in which the minority population in a given country is actually better off than the majority. The Chinese in Malaysia, for example, are better off than the Malay, which is the main reason large-scale policies of positive discrimination exist in the country: they are an attempt to improve the Malay majority's access to opportunities. Similarly, the Hungarian minority in Romania is often seen as better off than the majority Romanian population, despite past policies that have not always provided the Hungarian-populated region with its fair share of infrastructure. The Bamilekes in Cameroon are often considered better off than the rest of the population as a partial result of the very effective social capital that interconnects these traders, allowing them to use a wide range of social networks. Most familiar of all, of course, is the situation in South Africa, where colonial rule followed by the strong apartheid system left the white minority population better off than the majority African population.

last 10 years, with the single exception of China, where the gap is closing for the Han population.

In Latin America, about 30 percent of the population is of African origin or indigenous to the continent. These groups are disproportionately represented among the poor and comprise the large majority of people living in extreme poverty. In the middle of the 1990s, the national poverty rate in Guatemala was about 64 percent; this figure was 87 percent for the indigenous population. Similarly, in Peru, the general poverty rate was about 50 percent, but close to 80 percent for the indigenous population. The disproportion is particularly striking in Mexico, where the rate of poverty for the general population is a relatively low 18 percent, but is 81 percent among indigenous groups. These trends from the 1990s persist (Hall and Patrinos 2009).

In Asia, where ethnic minorities are numerous, many are worse off than the majority population, although supporting statistical data are scarce; this has sometimes led, as in Myanmar, to open conflict with the central government. In Vietnam, several poverty analyses conducted by donor agencies and the government over the last 10 years show that 14 percent of the population is comprised of members of 53 officially recognized ethnic minority groups, which account for 29 percent of the nation's poor. The poverty rate for these minorities is being reduced, but at a slower rate than for the Hink majority population.[6]

A variety of historical factors partially accounts for why minorities tend to be poorer than the majority population. Many minorities have been colonized or conquered. They have endured purposeful policies of oppression and attempts to destroy their culture and economic livelihoods. These factors are in many cases still discernible in the form of voluntary or involuntary discrimination. Such discrimination can be related to the marginal status of the population or cultural prejudice; it can also stem from a majority group's efforts to retain control over national assets and resources. Whatever the reason for discrimination, it is often manifested through stigmas linked to morphology (in particular, skin color), to cultural habits and practices, or simply to the minority's ethnicity or religion itself.

Another reason minorities are often overrepresented among the poor may derive from the difficulties of practicing a different culture than the majority. For instance, if the minority speaks a different language than the majority, minority students are at a disadvantage when learning to read and write in school; they may also feel disconnected from the history and geography presented in the curriculum. These barriers might also prevent them from getting support from their parents, who may have been educated in a different school system or no system at all. In some ways, these are examples of involuntary discrimination on the part of society at large. To be effective, any poverty reduction policies that deal with these issues will require not only a formal recognition but also a solid understanding of cultural factors.

Impact on Agency

Taking culture into account in public policy making can have a positive impact on collective and individual agency (see box 2.3 for a definition of this term). Few systematic studies have been undertaken on the impact of active cultural recognition on a population's well-being, given that the intrinsically subjective nature of the issue does not easily lend itself to measurement. However, philosophy professor Charles Taylor provides a clear articulation of how cultural recognition affects agency:

> The thesis is that our identity is partly shaped by recognition or its absence, often by misrecognition of others and so a person or a group of people can suffer damage, real distortion, if the people or society around them mirror back to them a confirming or demeaning or contemptible picture of themselves. Non-recognition or misrecognition can inflict harm, can be a form of oppression, imprisoning someone in a false, distorted, and reduced mode of being. Within this perspective misrecognition shows not just a lack of due respect. It can inflict a grievous wound saddening its victims.... Due recognition is not just a courtesy we owe people. It is a vital human need (Taylor 1994, p. 25).

This view is very much in line with recent social and anthropological studies that underscore the importance of society's recognition of a person's identity in enabling positive interactions with others (Jenkins 2008).[7]

Although it is difficult to measure the relationship of recognition to social inclusion and positive agency, a number of cases offer evidence of such a relationship. In New Zealand, a country with demonstrably successful integration policies, the recent improvement in the minority population's standard of living is closely correlated with an important renewal of interest in the Maori culture (Ringold 2005). It should be noted that it is not just the Maori who are experiencing a renewed interested in their own culture, but also the national majority as well.

Culture is also important to agency because of the influence it has on social capital. Interactions among people are strongly influenced by their culture. The French sociologist Pierre Bourdieu (2001) uses the notion of *habitus* to describe how the cultural environment in which one is born and raised will strongly define, among other things, the network of relationships in which a person lives and interacts over the course of his or her life. The study of social capital shows to what extent it is embedded in a culture. Many of the mechanisms that help people deal with security at the informal level are very often part of a local culture. The African tontine (rotating saving scheme) is another example of a system that usually works among people of the same cultural group.[8] Culture can also in some cases reduce agency if, to use social capital terminology, it gives preference to bonding relationships and does not form relationships with other groups or formal institutions. This type of social capital can isolate the group and reduce choice and opportunity.

Conflict Reduction

Understanding and promoting the cultural attributes of minority groups can reduce conflict. Group identity is defined in large part by the identification of similarities with and differences from others. This process of identification brings sociocultural groups together, reinforcing their internal cohesion. At times, groups of people will play out their differences to reinforce their identity, which is not necessarily negative. Sporting events, for example, elicit such behaviors, while at the same time—in most cases—reinforcing social cohesion. Conflict between different sociocultural groups should be seen as part of normal social interactions as long as it does not result in violence, discrimination, or exclusion. Both the state and civil society should help manage these conflicts so they do not erupt in any major way. To this end, it is useful to reinforce the commonalities among various groups, encourage respect and tolerance for differences in society, and emphasize the positive aspects of multiculturalism. These actions cannot be accomplished by negating the differences between groups, but rather by understanding these differences and providing a positive outlook on what they offer society as a whole.

Identity conflicts are often triggered by economic or political factors (power and control). They very rarely occur simply for cultural reasons.

The Risks of Taking Culture into Account in Developing Public Policy

Many policy makers and academics have cited the potential risks of taking culture into account in public policy, even if it is increasingly accepted that the benefits of culturally sensitive policy making outweigh the negatives. The potential drawbacks include the following:

- *Reduced autonomy and freedom of choice for some subgroups.* This argument is often made when discussing gender issues. It is argued, and rightly so, that some cultural practices favor the subordination of women. Polygamy, excision, the failure to send girls to school, or the failure to consult women on important decisions are often cited as negative aspects of some cultures. These practices keep women subordinated inside a group and go against principles of equity and freedom. Some cultures also support a strong age-based hierarchy (for example, councils of elders) and thus exclude youth from decision making, thereby reducing their capability. In some cases, hierarchical class structures embodied in local cultures encourage social exclusion. Examples include the caste system in India and in some African societies.[9]
- *Perpetuation of unfair and ineffective institutions.* Acknowledging and cooperating with local institutions that are part of a community's cultural tradition (as discussed in the next chapter) can perpetuate ineffective and unfair structures. Some cultural institutions, while important for maintaining social cohesion inside a group, do not promote behaviors that are conducive to economic or social development. For example, in Sub-Saharan Africa, entrepreneurs often complain that they cannot save money or resources because the pressure to share and redistribute these resources inside one's community is extremely strong. Because local institutions such as councils of elders or religious and traditional fraternities reinforce this pressure, they reduce an individual's ability to save and reinvest in a business. In Latin America, the use of traditional forms of indigenous government in communities has been criticized in some cases for supporting nepotism and corruption (Recondo 2007).
- *Isolation of communities from majority culture.* Critics charge that recognizing cultural practices and institutions when designing public policy tends to isolate specific groups from the majority population and therefore reduces the opportunity group members have to interact with the larger society. The practice can favor strong social networks specific to one group and embedded in one's culture and undermine the ability of this group to create networks and social interactions with other groups which are essential to reduce the risk of conflict and increase economic opportunities. It is also argued that recognizing cultural differences in

the public sphere will weaken the concept of citizenship, which is the main integrating factor in nation-states.

The risks represented by these arguments can be mitigated so that the benefits of taking cultural diversity into account in public policy will far outweigh them. To this end, public policy developers should keep the following points in mind:

- *Culture and tradition are not set in stone.* Even in the most closed societies, culture evolves and changes with the experience of the individuals in the community or through contact with other societies. Lévi-Strauss found, even in highly isolated indigenous populations such as that of the Brazilian Matto Grosso and Amazon provinces, evidence of cultures influencing and borrowing from each other. He saw evidence too of diversification from inside a culture and found that the more a culture involves a large population, the more it will diversify (Lévi-Strauss 1952). Thus, culture can change, societies can adapt, and some will in the process give greater voice to youth and women.[10]
- *Failure to recognize culture will not obliterate negative institutions.* Ignoring the negative systemic practices of minority cultures does not make the problem go away. Rather, these institutions will continue to operate informally in parallel, which could be even more detrimental for its members as they are isolated even further from mainstream society. For example, in many Sub-Saharan African countries, polygamy has survived and is even spreading, despite the fact that the countries do not officially recognize the practice. Here, the first marriage is considered the official one, but the following marriages are not civilly recognized, thus depriving these wives and any children they produce of formal legal protection.

Notes

1. Sembène Ousmane, the Sengelese "father of African film," vividly depicts the attractiveness of urban centers in distancing oneself from the pressure of local communities in his films *Xola* (1974), *Ceddo* (1977), and *Moolaadé* (2004).
2. For instance, article 27 of the International Covenant on Civil and Political Rights reads: "In those states in which ethnic, religious or linguistic minorities exist, persons belonging to such minorities shall not be denied the right, in community with the other members of their group, to enjoy their own culture, to profess and practice their own religion, or to use their own language."

3. For a detailed discussion of European recognition of cultural diversity, see Thomberry (2001).
4. According to Loury (2004, p. 26) self-confirming stereotypes are formed through the following sequence of events: (1) rational statistical inference in the presence of limited information, (2) feedback effects on the behavior of individuals due to their anticipation that such interferences will be made about them, and (3) a resulting convention "equilibrium" in which mutually confirming beliefs and behaviors emerge out of this interaction. Loury offers the example of taxi drivers who do not pick up black passengers because they are stereotyped as criminals. As a result, blacks stop trying to hail taxicabs. After a while, the only blacks that continue to hail taxis are criminals, and therefore the stereotype is self-confirming.
5. For more on the Indian experience with affirmative action, see Sabbagh (2003).
6. For more information, see CIE (2002), Guewardena and Van de Walle (2000), and Hall and Patrinos (2009).
7. See the appendix for a definition of cultural identity.
8. Tontine effectiveness also seems to be linked to gender; the system works much better among women than among men.
9. Certain African societies are strongly hierarchical, with rigid class structures. The Mauritanian society is strictly divided into warriors, religious leaders, artisans, and slaves; these categories determine lifelong opportunity and choice. A similar situation exists in various Sahelian cultures (Touareg, Peulh, and Goran, for instance, or some societies of South Africa). For more on the influence of the caste system in political participation, see Jaffrelot (2005).
10. In this regard, it should be noted that not all values of minority cultures are at odds with those of the majority. For example, despite its rigid class structure, Mauritanian society allows women great autonomy. In fact, a Mauritanian woman is more likely to be fully accepted by society following a divorce than her counterpart in many European countries.

CHAPTER 3

Cultural Diversity and Service Delivery

This chapter seeks to highlight the numerous, complex, and nuanced connections between cultural diversity and services delivered at the community level so that these can be taken into account when designing culturally sensitive policies and programs. Of the many services delivered at the community level, this chapter focuses on education, health, and cultural services, because these are strongly influenced by culture. This does not mean that other services should not be considered when designing policies that support cultural diversity: values, habits, and customs can affect the use of water, slaughterhouses, and roads, to name just a few.

The chapter also looks at how traditional governance systems (councils of elders, traditional courts, religious fraternities) can be used to deliver services.

Education

School is where a child's social identity is shaped and where future citizens are formed. It is therefore no coincidence that demands for recognizing cultural diversity are strongest in the field of education; the response has been the promotion of multicultural education.

Multicultural education is a broad term that includes teaching in languages other than the majority one, adapting curriculum to reflect the history and culture of minority groups, offering support to minority students when they are facing challenges that result from their cultural specificities, and making pedagogy more in step with cultural considerations. The supporters of multicultural education argue that it is consistent with today's efforts to improve the outcome of education systems across the world. "The accommodation of diversity in the educational system is also fully consistent with the 'outcome based' educational practices that researchers agree are needed if societies are to achieve sustainable social and economic development in our globalized world" (Smith 2006). In multicultural education, the main challenge is to create structures that support the development of a student's group identity while fostering common ground among groups that are part of the broader society. At the same time, it must efficiently instill in students skills that are useful in the labor market.

In the last decade, multicultural education has become increasingly popular, with notable expansion in Latin America and Eastern Europe. In Sub-Saharan Africa, multicultural education is still limited, even though the majority of children have a native language other than the official tongue.[1] Asia has also experimented with multicultural education, with notable results in Papua New Guinea (box 3.1), the world's most linguistically and culturally diverse nation.

It is important to understand both the nature of the demand for multicultural education and what forces drive it. Multicultural education usually has a strong ideological appeal and is often pushed by elites for political reasons. This may not be considered negative, as elites have often been at the forefront of social change; however, such reforms need to be understood and accepted by the intended beneficiaries at the local level. Moodley (2001), in considering multicultural education in Canada, maintains that it often overlooks the prime goals of equality of opportunity and

---

BOX 3.1

Success of Multicultural Education Reform in Papua New Guinea

In 1993, the Department of Education of Papua New Guinea implemented educational reforms that introduced native language instruction for the first year of school. By 2001, 369 indigenous languages were introduced in the program, and a third of elementary schoolchildren began education in their native tongue. Although the success of the program is largely anecdotal at this point, it has demonstrably increased educational access and resulted in a lower dropout rate, particularly among female students. Lower secondary school enrollments have doubled, and upper secondary numbers have quadrupled over the decade following the introduction of the reform (Litteral 2004).

equality of condition. She emphasizes that competence, not culture, is the main concern of minority parents, who often prefer to see their children learn a curriculum of basic skills in subjects needed to survive in the nation, rather than being taught fragmented versions of their culture by people with very little knowledge and understanding of it.[2] As a result, the study of multicultural education often tends to be overly politicized and sometimes ideologically driven, which makes evaluation of its impact difficult. This section attempts to provide a brief overview of the various issues and debates surrounding multicultural education.

Native Language Instruction

It is difficult to discuss education without examining a country's language policies and how it relates to nation building and the formation of citizenship. Language is arguably the most important vehicle of a culture. As Kymlicka and Grin point out,

> …when a language group fights to preserve its language, it is never just preserving a tool for communication: it is also preserving certain political claims, autonomous institutions, cultural products and practices, and national identities. Conversely, of course, when the state attempts to impose a dominant language on minorities, it is never just imposing a language: it is also imposing a set of political and cultural claims about the primacy of the state, the need for common rules and centralized institutions, the need to learn new history and literature and the construction of new nation-state loyalties and identities. Language disputes are never just disputes over language (Kymlicka and Grin 2003, p. 11).

It is clear that people have a wide range of interests in language, and, at least in a democratic society, it is necessary to accommodate these interests. At the same time, it is legitimate to want all members of a nation to be able to communicate easily with each other and to enable the state to interact with its citizens effectively.

Language policies touch on another highly important national interest: security, particularly for countries with weak national integration (as in Africa), or with contested borders and a history of strong central control (as in Eastern Europe and China). In such countries, both the government and the majority population often fear that granting language rights will reinforce cultural identity and encourage minorities to request autonomy or secede, thereby depriving the majority population of such benefits as, for example, access to natural resources or a particular territorial advantage.

From an educational viewpoint, instruction conducted in a student's native language has largely been recognized as an effective strategy in terms of cognitive development and the ability to learn other topics. A World Bank study concluded that, when learning is the goal, including learning of a second language, the child's first language should be used as the medium of instruction in the early years of schooling. The first language is essential for the initial teaching or reading and for comprehension of subject matter. It is the necessary foundation for the cognitive development upon which acquisition of the second language is based (Dutcher and Tucker 1997). Similarly, Mehotra (1998) finds that bilingual education, particularly at the early childhood level, supports cognitive development that aids in all aspects of later learning. Other evidence (UNESCO 2003) suggests that learning in one's native language increases interest in school participation and encourages school enrollment and attendance (box 3.2).

Adapting the Curriculum to Reflect Various Cultures

Teaching local languages at school is only one aspect of multicultural education. Another important component is the introduction of minority cultures in the broader school curriculum. Minority achievements and contributions should be taught in history, geography, and literature as well as with regard to music, art, and trade skills. How curriculum should be adapted to best reflect the various cultures of a country is a matter of debate, especially in nations with a history of conflict between these

---

BOX 3.2

Maori Immersion Education and Education Outcomes

The New Zealand government's 1982 introduction of Maori Immersion Education (education in the Maori language) has been successful in a variety of ways. First, it has grown to the extent that it is now possible for students in New Zealand to attend Maori language education from preschool through primary and secondary schools. In addition, it has created an incentive for other schools to start teaching Maori. It is estimated that 80 percent of Maori children learn their native language to various degrees and in various forms at the primary and secondary levels of education (Ringold 2005). According to evaluations carried out in New Zealand, the extension of Maori language education seems to have strongly affected students' ability to perform in class; no in-depth assessments on this finding have yet been carried out.

cultures. Some argue that incorporating minority culture into a curriculum can actually increase the sense of "otherness" regarding that culture; for example, drawing attention to a particular group through separate books and classes may tacitly reinforce the idea that this group does not belong to the majority. Such an outcome would undermine rather than strengthen social cohesion. For this reason, books and curricula that actually integrate the geography, history, arts, and achievements of a nation's various groups are preferable (Greaney 2006).

Curriculum adaptation is linked to a debate over pedagogy, as many specialists argue that culture informs not just the way a person learns, but also what a person is better suited to learn. Pedagogical concepts are embedded in culture and guided by the specific educational priorities and goals of a given society. They are reflected in models of generating and transmitting knowledge and skills, and in teaching methods and learning styles (King and Schielmann 2004). Ringold (2005) mentions that during her field visits in New Zealand, teachers commented that Maori students are more active and visual learners, and hence need to be treated differently in the classroom. This argument is also often made in the case of Roma children in Eastern Europe. However, teaching strategies that assume that certain students are predisposed to visual, tactile, or other types of learning also have the potential to increase segregation in the classroom by differentiating teaching methods and materials according to the cultural background of the student. This issue requires more study and analysis.

Taking Cultural Differences into Account in the Classroom

Successful multicultural education needs to center on the classroom because this is where social interactions occur among children, between children and teachers, and—especially—among children of different socioeconomic and cultural backgrounds. Different options exist for supporting the integration of children from minority cultures:

- Minorities could be taught in separate schools at the primary level to facilitate the teaching of their specific culture and avoid in-class discrimination.
- All students could be housed in the same school but taught in separate classrooms.
- All students could be taught together and learn the same things.

Which of these options is best is a matter of heated debate among specialists of multicultural education.

Hungary, which has made aggressive efforts in the area of multicultural education, supports three types of schools: schools in which classes are taught entirely in the minority language, bilingual schools in which both the national official language and the minority language are taught, and schools in which the native language is taught as a foreign language. The Hungarian system of education is quite decentralized, and many schools have room to adapt the noncore curriculum (that is, the curriculum that is not centrally defined by the Ministry of Education). Because the development of multicultural education is still relatively new, it is difficult at this stage to assess the merits of these different approaches.

There is serious debate regarding whether separate schools actually benefit minorities. In some countries—including Australia, New Zealand, and Slovak Republic, as well as several Latin American countries—minorities have historically attended separate schools or been made to attend special schools because language barriers made it difficult for them to follow lessons in majority schools. Such was the case for the Roma population in Eastern and Central Europe, for example. However, the schools Roma are made to attend were originally created for children with disabilities, thereby reinforcing the stereotype of Roma intellectual inferiority (box 3.3). Moreover, separate schools around the world are frequently second-rate (or worse) institutions, characterized by poor financing, isolation from mainstream education, and lower quality teachers, making learning of any kind

---

BOX 3.3

Institutionalized Discrimination: Segregated Schooling for the Roma

On November 13, 2007, the Grand Chamber of the European Court of Human Rights ruled, by a vote of 13 to 4, that segregating Roma students into special schools is a form of discrimination that violates fundamental human rights. The decision is the culmination of an eight-year legal battle between parents of children who were enrolled in special schools for children with mental disabilities and the Czech state. The judgment may have the same significance for Roma children as the 1954 *Brown v. Board of Education* case had for the integration of African-American children in U.S. schools. The European judgment is significant because it ruled that an education system can be discriminatory and in violation of Article 14 of the European Convention on Human Rights, even if there were no specific acts of discrimination by any individual (Roma Education Fund 2007).

difficult (Rossell, Armor, and Walberg 2002). Consequently, the idea of special schools for minorities is today often regarded very skeptically.

Other schools, especially primary schools, have had more success in supporting the education of minorities and catering to their specific cultural needs. The Maori language immersion schools in New Zealand resulting from the Kohanga Reo movement are an example of such success. The movement began with the goal of preserving the Maori language, teaching cultural traditions, transferring knowledge across generations, and providing education within a Maori cultural context. This experience has been met with at least some success, even if a real evaluation can be made only in the long term.

The preferred approach to multicultural education is to teach diverse groups of students together, but to use facilitators, teaching assistants, and special classes to address culturally sensitive curriculum. This method has been shown both to recognize that minority students have special needs and preferences and to ensure that they are not educated differently from the mainstream student body. It is helpful to offer after-hours sessions where students can receive help with specific curriculum related to minority culture and receive support to better keep up with in-class demands.

Bringing Cultural Diversity to Preschool

Preschool is seen as vital to socialization and helps prepare children for primary education. If approached as a transitional experience, preschool can play an important role in creating a peaceful and accessible bridge between minority and mainstream culture (box 3.4). For example, preschool education is seen as the most effective way to ensure that Roma children are successfully included in the European education system.

Maintaining Quality in Multicultural Education

The objective of multicultural education is to ensure quality education for minority languages and other curriculum. Such an endeavor is fraught with challenges. Delivering quality multicultural education usually requires funding additional teachers and textbooks, finding qualified teachers with a solid understanding of minority culture, coordinating between central and local authorities to implement the new curriculum, helping parents and children of the majority population understand the need for and purpose of the curriculum, and establishing a monitoring system to facilitate assessment of the curriculum's impact.

BOX 3.4

Social Inclusion and Preschool in Albania and Kosovo

The United Nations Children's Fund (UNICEF) and a local nongovernmental organization jointly launched a preschool program in Albania and Kosovo. The project was scaled up with financing from the World Bank and is focused on organizing community centers for mothers and their children of preschool age. The program was meant to benefit children who live in relatively isolated communities and are often confined to their homes due to violence and blood feuds (especially in northern Albania). The program has succeeded in getting mothers to accept the idea of schooling and socializing their children with those from other communities within the security of their mother's presence.

The situation varies considerably by case. Very often, the more isolated and marginalized a community, the more difficult it will be to introduce a new curriculum into the classroom. The effort will usually require comprehensive approaches that involve reforming or adapting many aspects of the educational system. In 2001, the Romanian government adopted a set of programs to focus exactly on these shortcomings. It included affirmative action to support Roma university enrollment; measures to increase the number of Roma-qualified teachers; outreach programs to stimulate interest in Roma studies; the design of curricula, textbooks, and didactic materials for the study of Roma language, history, and traditions; and the recruitment of Roma school inspectors to monitor the quality of Roma education and assess the implementation of the program.

Some circumstances will affect both the cost and quality of such programs—for example, whether the minority is geographically concentrated or dispersed throughout the country. Countries usually require a minimum concentration of children to start a bilingual education program. In Bulgaria, for example, a minimum of 13 students is required to appoint a teacher to a language class. If a minority is well organized, and has the support of neighboring nations (as is the case for the Hungarians in Romania, for instance), these obstacles become less challenging. Experience shows that motivated nongovernmental organizations (NGOs) can help in this area. In fact, the successful language immersion program of the Maori in New Zealand started with support from an NGO and then spread with the help of government funding.

All too often, the groups most in need of multicultural education—those that are marginal and poor with high illiteracy rates—are also the ones for which it is the most expensive and difficult to implement multicultural education. On the one hand, the German, the Hungarian, and, to some extent, the Turkish minorities in Eastern and Central Europe can access bilingual education fairly readily in most areas where they live. On the other hand, the Maya and Gayrani peoples of Latin America, the Roma in Europe, the San in southern Africa, and the Batwa in central Africa have more difficulty in accessing bilingual education.

Parent participation is a key to the success of multicultural education, largely because all education continues at home through the interest and support of parents. Mechanisms that facilitate parent involvement, such as school boards, monitoring committees, and parent-teacher associations, are all essential to quality multicultural education. Several evaluations of Bolivia's bilingual education program identified organized participation as critical to the program's success because it has given meaning to and mobilized action in bilingual education in the country. The Educational Councils of Indigenous Peoples, defined by the Bolivia educational reform law of 1994, have demonstrated great potential in creating commitment at the local level. In New Zealand, the strong community ownership of the Maori language immersion program is seen as one of the most important ingredients in its success.

Parent participation is particularly important in places where it is difficult to persuade municipal governments and the majority population that multicultural education benefits the whole community. Sometimes, the beneficiaries themselves might be skeptical of the benefits of multicultural education and what it can offer their children (box 3.5). A close dialogue between school management and educational staff is essential so that implementation of reforms can take into account the perceptions and reactions of the local population.

The participation of stakeholders other than parents is useful in developing multicultural education as well. Local governments and teachers can feel intimidated by education reform, especially when it has the potential to change a community's power structure. In Latin America, for example, teacher unions have often opposed multicultural education; they see the recruitment of indigenous and local minority teachers as a threat to both their job stability and control. Strong parent and community support for reforms usually helps counterbalance the reluctance of conservative teacher unions.

BOX 3.5

Considerations in Bilingual Education

When assessing the impact of bilingual education, one must take into account how interested a child is in learning a second language. This interest depends on issues of identity and the relevance of the second language. If the second language is seen as the language of the invader, as was the case for Russian in Baltic states under the Soviet Union, then not much energy will go into learning it (especially if a person can get by in society without mastering it). This will also be the case if a person doubts the second language will improve their livelihood. In Romania, members of the Hungarian minority often imagine themselves migrating to Hungary or another European Union country at some point in time—these goals, understandably, do not encourage families to teach their children Romanian.

Health Care

Recent literature attributes the poor health of indigenous populations and some minorities partially to a lack of awareness by the medical establishment of cultural issues and partially to the cultural environment in which the patient understands the illness and the cure. Researchers at the London School of Hygiene and Tropical Medicine in London argue that addressing the indigenous health crisis requires a more holistic vision of health research and interventions. Health services, they say, should be integrated with an indigenous view of health and well-being. They also advocate continued research on the health status of indigenous peoples, especially on incorporating indigenous perspectives on health into the design of health policies (Stephens and others 2005).

In designing health care policies, cultural considerations go beyond recognition of a country's specific minority and indigenous populations. In the United States, the concept of "cultural competence" was first developed in the 1980s by mental health researchers to deal with the lack of attention given to culture in treatment. They defined this concept as a set of congruent behaviors, attitudes, and policies that come together in a system or agency or among professionals that enables systems, agencies, and professionals to work effectively in cross-cultural situations. This basic concept has since been adopted throughout the medical community and promoted by the U.S. Department of Health and Human Services.

The concept of cultural competency goes beyond cultural awareness or sensitivity. It represents the institutionalization of efforts to provide appropriate programs or policies for diverse populations. A number of cultural competency techniques have been identified in the United States that could potentially be used to decrease racial and ethnic disparities in health care; these include interpreter services, recruitment and retention policies, training, coordinating the use of community health workers with traditional healers, culturally competent health promotion, the inclusion of family/community members, immersion in another culture, and administrative and organizational accommodation.

Health care policies that take cultural diversity into account have two main components. The first consists of measures aimed at recognizing the cultural background of a patient; the second consists of recognizing the value of a population's traditional curative practices. These components can be combined, but usually health care programs designed to reach minority groups with strong cultural specificities focus on the first component alone. Taking cultural diversity into account in the health care context is consistent with recent trends in public health that emphasize favoring preventive approaches over curative medicine, and outreach and general practices over hospital care.

Recognizing the Cultural Background of Patients

Recognizing the connection between health and culture—the way values and social norms inform the way people see their physical health—is seen in many reforms of health care systems as essential for effective outreach and acceptance of medical care, and to make prevention and cure more effective. Many surveys show that lack of trust in the Western health care system, together with the high cost of treatment, is an important issue in the developing world (Bhopal 2007).

Experience indicates that policy makers and practitioners need a better understanding of the relationship of wellness and illness to the body and mind in a specific culture. Many cultures do not view the mind and body as separate, as in Western medicine. Accounting for these philosophical differences entails both hiring health care workers who come from that particular culture and ensuring that other public health specialists and personnel understand what cure and wellness mean in specific cultural contexts. Because language can be a prohibitive barrier to health care, it is also essential that health care personnel speak the language of the minority group, especially in areas where knowledge of the national language is limited.

Respect for the cultural particularities that inform a person's relationship with his or her body should be integrated into the public health system. Notably, such integration should take gender issues into account. In some societies, for instance, it is not acceptable for a woman to see a male doctor, and vice versa. Other cultural dictates, such as being separated from one's family, eating food prepared outside the home, and being unable to perform prayers, can be major obstacles to accepting a health care system. A corresponding problem faced by health care systems is that some of these practices might violate the health care industry's hygiene standards; in such cases, some trade-off needs to be made.

Australia has made important inroads in adding cultural awareness to the training of doctors and nurses who work in aboriginal health care (Beaton 1994). Similarly, in 2001, the New Zealand Ministry of Health launched its Maori Health Strategy (He Korowai Oranga). The strategy identifies a range of factors beyond simple health services that determine health outcomes, including socioeconomic conditions, environment, social and community influences, diet, risk factors, gender, and culture. One of the main innovations of the strategy is the introduction of Maori health providers, who are contracted to deliver services to the Maori population under the framework of the Maori governance and management structure; these personnel take Maori values and culture into account in service provision (Ringold 2005).

In Romania, the government has taken several measures to increase access to health care for Roma residents (box 3.6). These include actions that increase Roma participation in health insurance programs and pro-

---

BOX 3.6

Roma Health Mediators in Roma Communities

One of the most successful efforts aimed at improving the health care of Roma communities has been the introduction of Roma health mediators. This effort was started in 1997 by the Roma Center for Social Intervention and Studies NGO and was officially adopted by the government in 2001. The health mediators help ease communication and understanding between Roma patients and medical staff. They are also charged with informing Roma communities about their rights regarding access to health care. In 2005, health mediators were active in 150 communities and facilitated access to health care for 38,000 Roma (Andreescu 2005).

mote intercultural education for all categories of medical personnel. The government has also adopted affirmative action measures (such as scholarships and training programs) to benefit Roma in the health education system, hoping this will result in increased opportunities for Roma to become health care providers themselves.

Recognizing the Importance of Traditional Medicine

It is only recently that Western medical institutions have begun to pay attention to the important role traditional forms of medicine have played, and continue to play, in various parts of the world. It is now recognized that some practices, such as acupuncture, the use of medicinal plants, and manual therapies, can be very effective in the treatment of certain illnesses. Even some psycho-symbolic curative systems—such as shamanism in Asia, traditional healing in Africa, and exorcism in Europe—have been found to be effective in treating certain psychological disorders. The World Health Organization (WHO) stresses that traditional healing remains a vital part of the health care strategies of indigenous communities (WHO 2002). The report suggests that, as such, traditional healing should either be recognized as a parallel system, equal but separate (as in India), or be integrated into the education for and practice of mainstream medicine (as in Bhutan, China, and Vietnam). Many studies have documented how associating traditional healers with Western medical practices has helped facilitate patient healing, in part because of the effectiveness of treatments but also because traditional methods offer a psychological and symbolic support Western medicine usually lacks (Yoder 1982).

The WHO adopted a traditional medicine strategy for 2002–05 (WHO 2002). The strategy recognizes that traditional medicine is widely used and rapidly growing. The WHO estimates that in Africa, 80 percent of the population uses traditional medicine; in China, traditional medicine represents 40 percent of delivered health care. In Malaysia, an estimated $500 million is spent annually on traditional health care compared to about $300 million on allopathic medicine. In Ghana, Mali, Nigeria, and Zambia, the first line of treatment for 60 percent of children with malaria is herbal medicines administered at home (WHO 2002). The WHO concludes that two main reasons underlie the popularity of traditional medicine: it is accessible and affordable (compared with Western medicines), and it is embedded in wider belief systems.

In Africa, the recognition of traditional medicines and healers has been linked in part to the emergency created by the AIDS epidemic.[3] Effective outreach campaigns are hampered by the limited reach of the Western medical system in rural areas and the population's lack of trust in its cures, which are often seen viewed as foreign. In contrast, traditional healers are seen as effective promoters of practices that could decrease the AIDS epidemic. What is needed is strong collaboration between traditional healers and Western medical practitioners. In 2000, an African Regional Strategy on Traditional Medicine was adopted to respond to this challenge. The strategy was followed by a plan of action for the Decade of Traditional Medicine, which was adopted by the African Union in 2005. The plan clearly mentions the potential role traditional healers can play in the battle against AIDS (African Union 2005). Ministers of health further confirmed the role that traditional medicine can play in terms of health promotion, diagnosis, treatment, and prevention of disease, and declared 2001–10 the Decade of African Traditional Medicine.

Supporting Collaboration between Traditional and Western Medicine

The WHO traditional medicine strategy identifies several challenges for states in recognizing and collaborating with traditional medicine: the weakness of national policy and regulatory frameworks, poorly understood safety considerations, management of efficacy and quality issues, problems of access, and problems related to the rational use of traditional medicine. These challenges (and a variety of others; see box 3.7) must be taken into account in developing policies on the use of traditional medicine.

Encouraging collaboration between traditional and Western medicine raises many issues, not least of which involves differing perceptions about the nature of a human being and a human's relationship to sickness and disease. Traditional medicine views the human being as embedded in a symbolic and cultural environment; it tends to favor treatments that focus not on the body per se but on the relation of the patient to the environment. Traditional medicines seek an equilibrium of the mind, the body, and the environment and emphasize health rather than disease. Practitioners tend to focus on the overall condition of the patient rather than on any particular ailments or diseases from which he or she is suffering (WHO 2002). In contrast, the Western medical establishment has historically avoided such a holistic approach, and most medical school programs do not cover holistic medicine. Additional proof of the value of traditional medicine is currently being sought, although a number of good studies have already demonstrated its efficacy in specific circumstances. The WHO strategy supports

BOX 3.7

Traditional Medicines, Contemporary Issues

U.S. and European pharmaceutical laboratories are actively involved in the study of traditional medicinal plants in Latin America and Asia, often in collaboration with national research institutions. Many governments have signed collaborative agreements on this type of research, but little attention has been paid to the property rights of those communities knowledgeable about these plants. In response, a number of associations have been created to organize the preservation of traditional medicinal knowledge. For example, the Organización de Medicos Indígenas del Estado de Chiapas and the Consejo de Organizaciones de Medicos y Parteras Indígenas de Chiapas in Mexico actively promote recognition of the rights of traditional medicine. In the last decade, similar associations have developed around the world to further facilitate relations among traditional healers, the state, and the private sector.

Interest in medicinal plants has implications for biodiversity conservation as well. Many of these plants are rare and are grown in very circumscribed environments, and overharvesting can quickly result in extinction. For this reason, many research institutions are conducting detailed inventories of medicinal plants and creating informal policies of protection along with environmental safeguards.

an increasing effort to further research traditional medicines by putting them through serious medical trials.[4]

Another major concern involves the credibility and legitimacy of traditional healers, especially in urban centers where acculturation is strong. Traditional healers are usually known in the community and are under some sort of collective control. People know who healers receive their knowledge from, how effective they have been in curing members of the community, and how legitimate they are according to local tradition and institutions. However, people may appoint themselves as healers for economic or political reasons, without any community control or input; this is particularly true in urban centers where community control is often reduced, and community checks and balances have been eroded.

Traditional medicine can be effective in the field of psychiatry because of the highly symbolic and cultural nature of some psychological illnesses. However, some approaches to healing can have a negative impact on society, particularly those that involve or invoke witchcraft or ostracize affected individuals. Such conflicts tend to be worse in environments where acculturation is stronger, such as large urban centers. In the Republic of Congo, for example, street children have recently been accused of practicing witchcraft.

In many countries, referral systems are weakened by the lack of communication between Western caregivers and traditional healers. Without an effective system of referral, people might be dissuaded from using Western medicine, even when it is available. In contrast, when Western medicine is unreliable or of very low quality, some traditional medicine can be effective; again, referral is usually lacking. Ideally, practitioners of both types of medicines should coordinate with each other to offer clients reliable referrals. Medical doctors and nurses should be understanding and respectful of what traditional medicine can offer, and vice versa. To achieve this, more research is needed on both medicinal plants and practices that accompany the prescription of these plants by traditional healers. Some university and medical school curricula address traditional practices, as is the case in China, where acupuncture is studied in medical programs. In practice, the traditional and Western medical communities more often ignore each other rather than collaborate. This is an area where much more effort is needed, especially in organizing primary health care and outreach.

Cultural Services

Being able to express one's culture in collective manifestations such as festivals, dances, and religious and musical ceremonies, as well as through the preservation of local knowledge and cultural patrimony, is important for strengthening identity. Festivals are particularly important in this regard by providing a symbolic representation of a culture rooted in actual events and celebration. These various activities create bonds among members of a community, strengthen social capital, foster a sense of pride, and help achieve a collective recognition of one's identity.

Local governments can do much to support such cultural services, and indeed can benefit economically through their provision (for example, in terms of tourism generated). Local provision of cultural services to support collective identity is thus far an understudied subject. Most assessments have examined the efficacy of community participation in preserving cultural heritage and in the development of community-based tourism. Yet the nature of demand for cultural services at the local level, and how local governments answer these needs, is rarely studied. The literature review carried out for this book has shown that, with the exception of some NGOs that try to document this demand, very little has been done.[5]

How Local Cultural Services Can Strengthen Identity

The types of activities usually supported are (1) festivals, celebrations that feature music, dances, processionals, traditional sports, religious activities, and concerts; (2) exhibitions and shows; (3) classes in traditional dance, music, art, traditional sports, and local industries; (4) preservation of local heritage and monuments through museums displays, collections, local knowledge (such as tales and oral traditions), culinary traditions, local medicinal traditions, small traditional trade, crafts, cooking, and dress; and (5) local radio and television stations aimed at preserving a culture and specific identity. These activities are often promoted by associations, small development projects, and NGOs, but are best when they remain a living activity in the community. Others can be added, but these five categories cover the bulk of demand for cultural services.

These activities have an important economic element. Cultural industries can be highly lucrative, especially for isolated communities with few development options. The explosive popularity of tourism around the world—and in particular, of ecological and cultural tourism—has generated strong interest in cultural industries that come from remote regions, along with a fascination for "exotic" items produced in the developing world. Globalization has placed traditional craft trade among the world's fastest growing industries, providing millions of dollars in earnings to developing countries. For example, Kenyan and Burkina Be baskets can now be found all over Europe. Similarly, Morocco's growth has been fuelled by a sharp increase in demand for native craft items, resulting in a boom in cities such as Fez and Marrakech. Indian crafts are being sold everywhere in the world, creating huge opportunities for the poorer communities that produce them.

But this increase in trade raises significant property rights issues. For example, Navajo baskets are produced in Pakistan to be sold to tourists near the Navajo reservation in Santa Fe, New Mexico; Pakistan's production costs are half those of a Navajo artisan. Similarly, traditional Mayan pots are produced in a factory in Mexico City. A different property rights issue is illustrated by the case of the traditional Taiwanese indigenous music which was featured as part of an anthem for the Atlanta Olympic Games—without the musicians' knowledge.

Livelihood sustainability is another major issue that accompanies increased tourism. For example, tourists have flocked to Masai villages in

Kenya; as a result, the Masai have stopped taking care of their cows and fields because they can make much more money from posing for photos than they could earn from farming. This example shows in a small way how external interest in a culture has the potential to weaken that culture very quickly.

Several countries have proactively developed local-level cultural services. In Guatemala, for example, a national congress on cultural policies was organized following the election of President Alfonso Portillo Cabrera in 2000. Participants included all major NGOs, associations, and local and central governments. The conference produced guidelines for developing the country's cultural policies; it also defined cultural policy as that which is rooted in the cultural values, cosmologies, modes of behaviors, beliefs, and actions of the various peoples of Guatemala. The guidelines put forth a variety of recommendations for increasing local participation in cultural policies and programs (Davis 2004).

Another example comes from Australia, where the Ministry for the Arts and the Ministry for Local Government produced cultural planning guidelines to help local governments recognize the significance of culture in the community. The cultural planning tool stresses the value dimension of culture: relationships, shared memories, experience and identity, diverse backgrounds, values, and aspirations (Government of New South Wales 2006).

In Albania, one of the strongest demands heard from Roma associations during poverty assessment consultations was the creation of Roma cultural centers, places where Roma could organize activities around education, folk dance, music, festivals, counseling, and other cultural activities. The government discussed these demands in 2002, at the country's first large consultation on Roma issues (De Soto and others 2002).

Supporting Community Initiatives

Local government can play a strong role as facilitator and supporter of community initiatives, and as manager of potential conflicts that can arise when other cultures view these manifestations as too intrusive. Providing space, helping with logistics and organization, and providing a supportive legal and administrative environment are often the most necessary services a government can offer.

Commercializing a living culture is a risky endeavor that requires careful management. Here again, central—and local—governments have a key role to play. A first priority is to protect cultural property rights.

Governments should adopt a policy that ensures communities are entitled to a substantial share of the profits or other proceeds reaped from their traditions.

Private sector involvement is positive when it brings know-how and a network of connections and markets. If this involvement is not properly managed, however, it can deny the local population their share of economic benefits. This issue has been increasingly raised to government authorities and the private sector by community groups, associations, and local NGOs. People are at risk of missing out on the economic benefits their culture may reap if cultural property is not actively protected.[6]

An even greater risk for a local community is to face rapid acculturation under the pressure of tourism and to be irrevocably changed by the consumerist needs of the growing tourist industry. Tourists are often genuinely interested in the culture of the region they visit, but tend to lack awareness of the damage their visit can do. Craftsmanship is often eroded very rapidly by the strong commercial pressure to adapt to the demands of a different culture and the need to sell goods cheaply. Tourism can also generate abuse of, or a lack of respect for, sacred spaces and customs, and contribute to anti-foreigner feelings.

Local government has an important role to play in knowing what pieces of the local culture to share with tourists and which pieces to preserve for the local community only. An example of this comes from the Hopi Indian mesas in Arizona. While tourists are welcome, a large part of the village is off limits to them. Furthermore, tourists may only visit with a guide and are not allowed to be present for the most important ceremonies and rituals. Tourists are also banned from communities after a certain time of day. This is a good example of how local governments can ensure their community collectively benefits from cultural expression and assets, and how the negative effect of commercialization can be minimized.

Delivering Services through Traditional Local Governance Systems

Delivering services in multicultural environments usually raises the question of how to tap local community-based institutions and existing community-level traditional governance systems. On the one hand, making use of institutions that are embedded in the local culture helps preserve the cohesion of the group at the community level because people already understand and trust them; on the other hand, these systems might not be accepted by everyone in the community, might not be effective, and might be influenced by evolving power structures within their communities. Additionally, they might exclude some groups, as they tend to be patriarchal and to marginalize women, young people, and those who belong to lower castes or social groups.

The world has many examples of such institutions and systems, which serve such functions as delivering justice, mediating conflicts, organizing community work, organizing festivals and religious celebrations, and organizing and regulating trade. They are often used by central and local governments to administer small rural communities, distribute humanitarian assistance, ensure security, and manage certain basic services. Bolivia, along with several other countries, recently attempted to give a much larger role to these institutions in service delivery and to involve them in the implementation of large national programs (Waters 2007).

This section looks specifically at local community councils to illustrate both the advantages and risks of involving local institutions in service delivery.

The Role of Local Community Councils

One of the most common forms of local governance is the council of elders, which is generally charged with managing community life and essential services.

- In Albania, the *fis*—the council of elders who administered villages and, in some cases, urban communities—took on an increasingly important role to compensate for the collapse of such formal institutions as collective farms and municipal governments after the fall of the communist state (box 3.8). It also became responsible for administering justice and managing local conflicts in many areas of the country.
- In Madagascar, the *fokonolona*, a village council made up of elders and other local notables, became so important it was given constitutional recognition in 1975.
- In Indonesia in 1999, the provincial government of West Sumatra issued a regulation that reinstated the *nafgari* as the basic governing unit. Before being disbanded by Soeharto, the nafgari system had operated as the basic governance unit of the Minangkabau society in that region. The system's structure and function are quite democratic and clearly delineated; it regulates and implements both formal and traditional systems of governance through its general assembly of traditional authorities.

BOX 3.8

The Return of the Kanun and the Fis in Albania

An interesting case that illustrates reliance on local institutions and local customary law is the return of the fis and of the Kanun in northern Albania following the fall of the Albanian communist regime. Local communities there faced a massive collapse of state structures, and so resurrected the use of the Kanun, a body of customary law that had been partly collected and written down in the 14th century. The law is aimed at regulating relations among members of communities. The Kanun is implemented by the fis, which is comprised of the most respected and experienced men in the community. The Kanun has helped restore order and some economic activity, but has a major gender and age bias. Also, because it recognizes the right of revenge, it has actually led to the rise of blood feuds between some families and has fostered a culture of fear and suspicion, with many negative impacts on local development. Now that the state has regained its authority and some of its legitimacy, the Kanun is used less often but has not completely disappeared.

- Over the course of the 1990s, many Latin American countries recognized traditional governance mechanisms for indigenous municipalities. The system is based on the principle of duties of office (*sistema de cargo*). The most important decisions are made in village assemblies, and those responsible for various religious and civil functions are nominated by the assembly after deliberation.

Council members are not usually elected but rather are nominated after community discussions that are more or less open to all community members (the participation of women and youth varies greatly according to local custom). Nomination can reflect a person's importance in a clan or subgroup of the community, or important contributions to the community the person has made or can make. In many places, council members are also part of the community's religious life. In rural Africa, for example, many elders are part of secret religious societies. In Muslim countries, the local *mullah* will usually play a very important role on the council, as will the shaman and main officials representing local religions in Latin America.

Today, many councils have added new structures that permit the increased participation of women, youth, and important economic actors. In some cases, these take the form of new committees. In other cases, new members may be added to the council of elders under the influence of dynamic members of the community, government, or development agencies. Sometimes, these changes are introduced by development programs and are either rejected or slowly integrated by the communities. The Kecamatan Development Program in Indonesia, for instance, uses local informal councils for making decisions on the use of funds it provides to the communities, but has encouraged the creation of parallel women's groups that decide on the use of some of the funds for projects that are a priority for women (Guggenheim and others 2004). This approach was successfully replicated in the Afghanistan National Solidarity Program, the largest community-based program implemented in Afghanistan (World Bank 2009).

Sometimes, the traditional structure adapts and becomes a hybrid. In his analysis of electoral systems in Mexican communities, David Recondo has shown how traditional, custom-based governance systems can integrate the electoral principle of modern democracies:

> The constant exchange between traditional voting, in which consecration takes precedence over selection, and universal suffrage, secret and individual, proves to what extent election modes are neither instrumental techniques devoid of inherent values, nor the product of an ontological otherness that would make it impossible to embed them in differing cultural contexts (Recondo 2007, p. 178).

The configuration of village councils has certainly changed over time, even if rigid structures that are embedded in the culture—for example those in the Pacific islands—are not evolving as fast. Newly powerful religious groups, such as the Pentecostals in Latin America or Islamist groups in the Middle East, can further influence how local governance is structured and operates—in some cases, these emergent groups have even hijacked them. This is the case as well with political parties, such as the Partido Revolucionario Institucional (PRI) in Mexico that has, through its clientelist network, managed to control nominations at public functions in self-governing villages. In some cases, local governance systems have also been used by dictatorial regimes to bypass national democratic institutions. Because of the large spectrum of local governance mechanisms, it is difficult to draw more precise generalizations about their roles and structure.

Involving Local Councils in Service Delivery

In some cases, the state does not have much choice but to recognize traditional governance systems, especially if it cannot afford to develop a new bureaucracy in a remote region. Often, using local governance mechanisms to manage the needs of small communities is the safest and most cost-effective option when the government does not have the means to develop a new local apparatus. In countries where a large section of the population has limited access to basic services, using local institutions that have established credibility and proven functionality is the most cost-effective way of governing. Many states, such as Ethiopia, are not able to offer outreach to the whole country and therefore must rely on local systems.

If the traditional structure offers some continuity and at least some form of local checks and balances, it is more effective to use it than to create new structures, even if the government has the financial means to do so. Many English-speaking countries in the developing world, for instance, have continued the indirect rule tradition put in place by the British colonials of letting local matters be managed by local institutions. Ghana, for instance, has maintained the chieftain structure and has recognized it in its constitution even as it has strengthened local government structures. When the government has more effective services, as in Mexico, the use of local governance systems is seen as a way of ensuring fuller participation of groups with cultural specificity—that is, mostly indigenous communities.

Using local governance structures requires an understanding of the philosophy that underlies the management structure. Local governance systems are the organizational expression of societal values and, as such, represent a certain vision of power sharing by assigning specific roles to different members of society. They usually emphasize individual duties toward the community, which can be a very different emphasis than that of the nation-state system, which focuses on links between an individual and society at large (box 3.9).

It is often a mistake to assume that, once in place, local management structures will ensure the full participation of citizens and shield them from political and other external interests. There are many cases in which a community has been manipulated by outside forces, such as the state, political parties, religious groups, or other institutions that were not historically part of the community. When the local culture experiences rapid change, the community is often not strong enough to counteract such manipulation.

Using local councils to deliver services to the population usually requires a good political/economic assessment of the councils to determine

BOX 3.9

Local Governance versus National Citizenship in Totontepec, Mexico

In her study of management practices in Totontepec, a small Mexican town inhabited by the indigenous Mixe people, Morales (2005) describes an event that illustrates how local governance principles can clash with national citizenship. In 1982, Pascacio, a member of the Totontepec community, was nominated by an assembly of citizens to take responsibility for the village water committee, but he refused the job. According to the customary rules of local governance, the responsibilities are not remunerated; members of the community are obligated to donate their time. In a general assembly, the community decided that because Pascacio refused to fulfill his duties, he should be banned. Pascacio was denied access to his house and his land. He protested to the governor, pointing out that his treatment was in violation of his constitutional right to protect his individual property. When the head of the community was summoned by the regional governor and asked to let Pascacio reenter his house, the head refused; he said that the law allowed his community to self-rule, and Pascacio was in violation of custom. The issue was resolved, more or less, when Pascacio went to live in another community.

- how representative they are of the community members—in particular, their representation of women, youth, migrants, and lower caste and other social groups;
- the types of decisions and activities the local community entrusts to them;
- the alignment of their role, functions, and decision-making process with existing national legal systems and institutions (box 3.9 clearly illustrates the problems of a lack of alignment);
- their capacity and ability to understand the technical aspects of the activities they might be required to assume.

Notes

1. African languages are usually used as the medium of instruction in lower primary schools; several countries (Botswana, Ethiopia, Eritrea, Lesotho, Madagascar, Nigeria, Somalia, Tanzania, and Uganda) have reportedly extended African language instruction to middle and upper primary levels.

2. For a more in-depth understanding of the debate on multicultural education, see Banks (2001) and Webster (1997).

3. See Gibbal (1984) on the rapid development of traditional medicine in Africa.

4. In this regard, the WHO (2002) highlights a study undertaken by Peru's National Program in Complementary Medicine and the Pan American Health Organization, which compared traditional medicine and allopathic medicine practices through systematic follow-up of 339 patients for one year. Treatments of the following pathologies were analyzed: moderate osteoarthritis, back pain, anxiety-based neuroses, asthma, peptic acid disease, tension migraine headache, exogenous obesity, and peripheral facial analysis. The overall cost-effectiveness of traditional medicine was 53 to 63 percent higher than that of conventional treatments for selected pathologies.

5. Traditions for Tomorrow is one such NGO. It is a Swiss organization, with French and U.S. subsidiaries, which finances projects aimed at strengthening the cultural identity of local communities, mostly in Latin America. It was created in 1986 and finances small projects around the continent, responding to the needs of local groups and communities. According to its statutes, Traditions for Tomorrow works to improve dignity, self-esteem, and confidence in communities that will consequently be better positioned to take an active role in their own development.

6. For more on the topic of property rights and cultural traditions, see Posey and Dutfield (1996) and Coombe (2005).

Designing and Implementing Policies That Support Cultural Diversity in Service Delivery

It is difficult to come up with clear-cut policy recommendations for incorporating cultural diversity into service delivery. Impact analysis of the policies and programs that support cultural diversity is still very limited; also, this is a relatively new topic for governments and international organizations. Consequently, the best way to nurture cultural diversity at the local level while at the same time preserving cohesion, striving for equity, and avoiding conflict is still open to debate.

The nascent theory of multiculturalism states that recognizing and acknowledging cultural diversity will help achieve cohesion and equity, and its negation will do the reverse. This recognition must be carefully managed by governments, political authorities, and community members themselves. Culture and identity are highly volatile and must be handled with care. Actions that support cultural diversity must be integrated into general social and economic policies in order to be effective. The strategy is not to develop parallel policies, but to make cultural diversity a mainstream priority for government policies and programs. In short, cultural diversity is handled best when integrated into overall social and economic policies.

Countries are increasingly approving international treaties aimed at recognizing cultural diversity and are actively introducing the concept into their constitutions and overarching legal frameworks. These actions have been taken at the prodding of international organizations such as the UN, and have been guided by success stories emerging from such countries as Canada, New Zealand, and Spain (Kymlicka 1995, 2007). However, transforming these broad legislative frameworks into effective policies and programs for basic service delivery has proven problematic. This chapter provides some recommendations for the design of policies and programs regarding the delivery of basic services that take cultural diversity into account with the goal of increasing social cohesion and inclusion.

A Conceptual Framework to Guide Policies

When designing policies that nurture cultural diversity, it is important to make sure everyone involved has a common understanding of what culture *is*. As noted earlier, culture is not static; rather, it is always in a process of change and hybridization following contact with other cultures. These changes may occur quickly or slowly, but they are always ongoing. Globalization has accelerated cultural change, and this has affected all cultures. Today, it is impossible to completely isolate one culture from another, and increasingly, people tend to consider themselves cultural "hybrids." It is therefore essential to see individuals as being under the influence of multiple value systems rather than a single one. But it is also clear that people do not just adopt the culture they like. Culture is in large part a legacy of one's family and of the social structure under which one lives.

A particularly important aspect of a culture is how it defines relations between individuals (that is, the individual dimension of a human being) and others (that is, the collective dimension of a human being). Sociology teaches that a human being aspires both to stand alone, to be the master of his or her own destiny; and to be part of a larger group, to be in tune with others, to recognize and be recognized by others. These conflicting aspirations shape the inherent tensions inside a society: a person wants to be an individual, and yet wants to be part of others. All cultures offer ways to manage this tension, providing institutions that help balance these aspirations. Some focus more on the collective/group dimension, favoring the integrating factors; others focus more on individual aspirations, such as the freedom to choose and actualize one's own life. A culture may move between these two poles over time, but cultures tend to differ with regard to how they relate individual with collective aspirations.

The relationship between the individual and the collective has changed in recent history. The community, or collective, has been replaced by a much broader society in which most interactions between the group and the individual take place. This shift has accelerated since the advent of the Industrial Revolution. In a community, there is a direct relationship with all members of the group; people can actually have contact with every one in the community and can communicate one-on-one. Group members' individual aspirations are in large part defined by these interactions. When societies grow to the state or nation level, interactions with others in society change. Yet the collective dimension remains internalized in people's imaginations because, in practice, members of a society can never all meet together, and because power relationships are not personified but expressed in broad institutions.

This type of social organization has unleashed the individual aspirations of its members. Roles and positions are not set by others but are reached through competition, and in a much less personalized way than in a community. The European enlightenment philosophy has been an important milestone in this shift, formalizing key concepts such as human rights, democratic representation, and the nation-state in both its symbolic and pragmatic aspects. These concepts define the governments and policies that are now in place in most countries.

The enlightenment philosophers went far in thinking through the legal and institutional framework establishing a new relationship between individual aspirations and the group. The group is no longer the community, but has morphed into a society. As a result, the traditional symbolic events that brought community members together are replaced with symbolic events that create a collective imagination. This process gives the nation-state a reality of its own.

Today, the nation-state is increasingly considered just one societal reference for its people, who experience their symbolic references outside of this structure, even if the nation-state remains the defining framework for many policies, at least legally. This evolution has been described by some psychologists and sociologists as *individuation*—the growing importance of individual (human) rights, the freedom to shape one's own destiny within one's own lifetime, and the ability to decide what part of a group one wishes to join. Such thinking informs the movements that support, for example, equality between men and women, increased recognition of youth, and the recognition of minority rights.

These ideas may seem abstract, but they have strong relevance for policy making. Assessing how collective and individual aspirations are going to interact when institutions or practices from a specific culture are integrated in the delivery of services is an important first step for policy making. Understanding how these institutions and practices influence the power structure in a community—and, more broadly, the functioning of existing institutions—is critical.

The second step is to understand how different systems that express a society's cultural diversity will work together. Usually, these are not all based on the same set of values. The cases reviewed here show that contradictions often arise because some practices are not based on nationally shared values and visions of society. Social assessments can offer some understanding of these issues, but must go far beyond simply asking for opinions—they should also use observations to arrive at an understanding of the internal dynamic of a group and its interaction with the majority culture.

No Universal Solutions

Only the most incurably visionary analyst would claim that foolproof, universally applicable formulas for accommodation of ethnic diversity exist. Policy experiences resemble balance sheets, rather than triumphant lists of accomplishments; in all spheres we investigate, there are liabilities as well as assets. The cultural circumstances of given polities vary widely; the many small, localized ethnic identities of Papua New Guinea, for instance, bear little resemblance to the intensely mobilized ethno-national collectivities in former Yugoslavia (Young 1998, p. 7).

Crawford Young expresses a view that has been confirmed in the experiences reviewed here. World situations are too varied to establish a detailed universal framework for taking cultural diversity into account when delivering services. However, certain basic rules seem to apply:

- Culturally diverse policies should not be pursued from the top down only; they require a bottom-up approach as well.
- Policies cannot be driven solely by elites. The intended local beneficiaries, especially the poor, need to understand how these policies seek to improve their day-to-day lives.
- Cultural diversity cannot be solely a matter of law and its implementation; deep institutional changes are also required.
- Like any institutional reform, recognizing a minority culture is a process that must be managed over time. Cultures adapt and change, and flexible policies allow corrections and adaptations to be made along the way.

Understanding Political Motivations

When a country decides to recognize different cultures and shape its services accordingly, there are undoubtedly political motivations in play.

There are many reasons why political forces might want to support such an agenda, and some can be motivated by interests that actually go against those of the group(s) in question. For example, cultural diversity is often the target of populist agendas: because such policies touch on symbolic identities, they can create strong political division. It is therefore important that political motivations be clear, at least in the mind of the technocrats who design the policies.

A country's sense of itself in the world and in history can often provide a clue as to its political receptivity to cultural diversity policy development. Hungary, for instance, has moved aggressively to recognize the specific cultural identities of its minorities in terms of both service delivery and political representation. Its motivation has stemmed less from any internal problems encountered with its minorities, which are few in number and generally well integrated, but rather from a desire to protect and support Hungarian minorities in neighboring countries. Hungary could not advocate the case of Hungarian minorities abroad without providing a positive example of leadership in this regard in its own country. Turkey, on the other hand, has strongly resisted recognition of its minorities, which include not only Kurds but also Greeks, Jews, Orthodox Christians, and Alevists. This attitude is a legacy of the collapse of the Ottoman Empire, which fell apart mostly as the result of uprisings by its many minorities, supported more or less effectively by European nations. This context makes cultural diversity and the recognition of cultural rights a very difficult political issue in that nation.

It is important to see the problem of cultural diversity in terms of its political significance. An example comes from Guatemala, where underneath the issue of recognizing cultural differences lies the very delicate matter of inequitable repartitioning of land. Many Indian communities view this as straightforward spoliation. Trying to resolve the tensions among indigenous populations, whites, and *mestizos* by recognizing cultural diversity will not be sufficient. Policies that support more equal distribution of assets—in particular, land—will be essential.

Understanding political factors requires knowing the specific source of the demand for adapting services to local culture. Even though smaller, minority groups are no more homogenous than a given majority culture. In some instances, those advocating for cultural diversity may not represent the will of the community. An urban elite of a minority group may champion instruction in native languages on the basis of cultural continuity and tradition, while the main population is usually more pragmatic. Field surveys have revealed that parents want children to learn what is useful in the labor market and are skeptical of whether it is valuable to teach native languages in school (Moodley 2001). Policy makers should not assume that minority advocates are in tune with all members of their group.

Recognizing cultural diversity can create political opportunities for elites of a minority. This is not always a negative effect, but it can be so in political systems that tend to encourage nepotism and corruption. The PRI in Mexico has co-opted much of the indigenous leadership in this way. PRI behavior very rarely benefits the development of the population it represents. Solid analysis of the political economy of cultural diversity at the local level is thus essential prior to implementing cultural diversity programs; this is particularly true when using local governance systems for service delivery.

Integrated and Multisectoral Approaches

Making and implementing policies that effectively recognize cultural diversity spans multiple sectors and requires multiple products and programs. To take a simple example, creating educational environments that support a native language does not make much sense if the students will never use this language outside of narrow family circles; conversely, asking health workers to speak a local language that is not taught in schools is similarly futile. It is illogical to recognize customary law, but not the language in which the law is expressed and applied. Consequently, recognizing cultural diversity usually means working on a package of policies and services.

To be effective, cultural diversity must be integrated into comprehensive sectoral policies. For example, teaching the language, history, geography, and arts of a specific cultural group should be included in overall education policy and programs. Recognizing elements of customary law should be included in broader legal reforms, and recognizing local governance systems should be included in decentralization policies. All of these policies and programs must be coordinated so they work together for the benefit of the local population. This coordination is not easy, as some sectors move faster than others, or some might experience more resistance than others. All too often, policies and programs aimed at recognition of cultural diversity and cultural identity are designed in a piecemeal fashion.

When policies have been effective, they have usually been multisectoral and coordinated at the highest level of government. New Zealand is an interesting example of a government that has considerably improved the living standards of its indigenous population through an integrated and multisectoral approach. It has provided this support by combining policies that promote positive cultural recognition and active political participation with more traditional policies aimed at increasing access to social services and employment. As for political representation, in 1996, New Zealand reformed its electoral system to introduce a "mixed-member" proportional system. Consequently, the Maori have representation in the parliament, and are in fact today better represented on a per capita basis than the majority population.

Efforts in the field of education have had similarly impressive results. By 2003, 88 percent of Maori students entering primary school had attended some form of early childhood education or child care. In 1986, an estimated 47 percent of 16-year-old Maoris were in school; this increased to 63 percent by 2003—influenced also by an increase of the age at which students left school (from 15 to 16) in the early 1990s. In 2003, the share of Maori who left school without qualifications fell to 30 percent, down from 38 percent in 1990. Finally, tertiary education participation has expanded exponentially from 7 percent in 1998 to 20 percent in 2003.

The active labor market policies also proved fruitful, as Maori employment has rebounded from the recession of the early 1990s. More Maori are participating in the labor force, and unemployment has reached a record low of 8 percent. This was closely correlated with a revitalization of Maori culture. It has included increased support for Maori language and cultural development: today, 42 percent of Maori adults have some level of competency in Reo, the Maori language. Participation in Maori immersion schools and bilingual programs has increased, and, across the board, many local traditions have experienced renewal.

It is very difficult to show how each of these policies has contributed to the improvement of living standards for the Maori population. But it is clear that where the combinations of these three policies were implemented, between 1997–98 and 2003–04, the share of Maori with no or low incomes declined while the share with incomes above a peak level of $550 per week increased (Ringold 2005).

In Guatemala, where the 2002 peace accords enabled consideration for the first time of the indigenous population as a whole, the country tackled the issue by integrating virtually all relevant sectors (even if some were more contentious than others) and thereby created a set of improved and coherent policies to support the indigenous population.

Establishing National Frameworks for Managing Cultural Diversity

It would be a relatively simple matter to pilot demonstration programs addressing cultural diversity in service delivery at the local level. Yet such programs would not be effective without a clear policy and legislative framework in place at the national level to lend legitimacy and provide a solid basis to the initiative. Numerous organizations—including the UN, the Council of Europe, and the Organization of American States—have, as discussed in chapter 2, developed various treaties and conventions on cultural diversity. These provide a rationale, a set of reasons, for signatory countries in developing and adopting multicultural policies within a coherent and comprehensive framework of their own. Such a framework signals the national government's commitment to cultural diversity and provides an organizational tool for coordinating sectoral policies.

The issues involved in cultural diversity policy making—efforts to recognize customary law, introduce native language classes in public schools, recognize local governance systems, and so on—often require fundamental legal changes. These changes can be so sweeping that countries have had to modify or adapt their constitutions to accommodate them.[1]

For example, Romania, under pressure from the European Union and the Council of Europe, in 1989 launched a process for establishing a national framework to recognize cultural diversity. Various official documents were developed to establish directions for the government to

- contribute to the development of ethnic, cultural, religious, and linguistic identity;
- fight discrimination and promote tolerance;
- stress cultural diversity values;
- stimulate interethnic dialogue;
- eliminate any form of extremism, chauvinism, and anti-Semitism;
- improve the situation of the Roma population and continue to implement policies aimed at reducing social exclusion.

The government has been working on an overall legal framework to effectively support national minority institutions, along with a law to ensure that Romania is in line with the European Charter for Regional or Minority Languages. It is also working to create a legal framework for the use of local languages in decentralized state structures (Andreescu 2005).

Adaptation of a national legislative basis is rarely sufficient to ensure its implementation. In most cases, national institutions also need to be changed. To this end, some countries have created ministries or a state secretariat to oversee issues relating to minorities. Hungary, for example, has a state secretary for minority issues; New Zealand has a ministry for Maori development. Experience has shown, however, that issues related to recognizing cultural diversity seem to be best managed by the relevant sectoral ministries. For their part, specialized secretariats and ministries dedicated to minority affairs can be effective in developing multisectoral programs. They are also often better positioned to establish participatory mechanisms and interact with civil society and associations charged with minority issues. Some countries have established permanent commissions to design multicultural policies in accordance with an overall vision; this is the approach taken by the Peace and Reconciliation Commission in Guatemala. These multicultural institutions work best when they have the ability to assess the impact of policies on beneficiaries and report problems to the central government in a timely manner.

Establishing Clarity in Decentralization Frameworks

It is generally accepted that policies for cultural diversity are better implemented in countries with some degree of decentralization (Kymlicka 1995). However, without a strong push from central government, decentralization alone is likely insufficient to support cultural diversity, particularly as experience also shows that it is at the local level that stereotypes, stigma, and discrimination tend to be the strongest because this is the level at which day-to-day confrontations between cultures occur. For example, opposition to discrimination against lower castes in India was initiated and promulgated with major involvement from the central government, especially through civil service employment and rules on political representation in national assemblies. Regions built on this foundation, following up with effective local projects dealing with access to services.

The classic problems with decentralization need to be taken into account in making services more responsive to cultural diversity. These drawbacks include the lack of separation of responsibilities across various levels of government, the tendency to devolve problems to the local government without providing sufficient financial and institutional support for their resolution, and absence of local municipal management. Major bottlenecks at the local level in program implementation frequently derive from a lack of clear understanding of what is needed, along with little if any institutional support in terms of communication, advice, training, guidelines, capacity building, and financing. The World Bank's public expenditure review in Guatemala, for example, found that decentralization has helped services adapt to variations in local needs, tastes, and cultural traditions but has also led to increased inequality in the distribution of public services because poorer jurisdictions lack the institutional capacity and financial resources to manage new responsibilities effectively (World Bank 2005).

Another common problem is the lack of clear political will to implement national multicultural policies at the local level, especially when these aim to change the balance of community power. Where various communities live in the same territory and under the aegis of the same municipal or regional authority, some groups strongly resist the recognition of the cultural specificity of other minority groups. For example, many policies regarding Roma integration are blocked at the local level.

Involvement of Concerned Sociocultural Groups

Because policies and programs that support cultural diversity directly affect societal norms, values, and local power structures as well as influence relations between the individual and the group, stakeholder participation is essential to their successful introduction. There must be commitment to and support for these changes, and any communities that might be negatively affected by such policy changes should be compensated. Involvement of the relevant socioeconomic group can occur at a variety of levels throughout the process of making and implementing policy:

- The target beneficiaries can be consulted early on to determine their view of the service and delivery mechanisms; this can be performed through a variety of mechanisms including polls, surveys, and meetings.
- The target group can be engaged in a discussion aimed at reform of the service and its delivery, with various options presented and debated. This information can be gleaned through the same mechanisms as above or through referendum.
- Communities can be engaged in service implementation through traditional governance systems or various other mechanisms for participation.
- The relevant communities can be involved in the monitoring and evaluation of services once implemented. They can provide their feedback

and rate service delivery through such mechanisms as score cards, opinion surveys, or focus groups. Their input should be elicited regarding how to use the results of the findings.

The stakeholders that need to be involved in policy/program preparation include representatives from various levels of government and from different groups. At the national level, political representatives of various organizations, NGOs, and associations that represent minority interests must establish an active and ongoing dialogue. Countries that have developed a framework for multicultural policies usually also have established mechanisms that encourage participation and consultation at the national level. The Romanian constitution, for example, recognizes the right of ethnic minorities to be politically represented in the parliament. Similarly, in New Zealand, a quota of seats is reserved for Maori representatives. At the local level, processes that encourage participation will need to be introduced to draw in the relevant communities, NGOs, and governments.

Different forms of consultation can be used, as outlined above; many of these methods can be employed to ensure that all members of a community are involved. Also, traditional institutions and community groups can be used as a forum for these consultations. However, as discussed in chapter 3, many traditional institutions consider certain subgroups as not having equal status, with the result that women and younger community members are often denied a voice in local governance systems. Therefore, in using traditional consultative mechanisms to discuss multicultural policies and programs, efforts must be made to prevent women, youth, and other subgroups from being excluded. This might require using an institution in which they have a stronger voice, such as a women's or youth society; or ensuring that the community council becomes more receptive to the opinions of marginalized groups. In many cases, a new focus group will be needed to assess the views of marginalized groups.

Balance between Citizens' Rights and Cultural Rights

Designing policies and programs that nurture cultural diversity is a delicate process. It requires carefully balancing the protection of individual human rights with the recognition of collective cultural ones. A number of approaches can be followed to achieve this aim. To begin with, the participatory process and social assessments mentioned in the preceding section should be used to identify areas in which the recognition of cultural rights could result in a major barrier to individual rights. Participatory processes should also be used to determine how much people are willing to accept trade-offs when they exist. For instance, if customary law recognizes corporal punishment, it might be possible to substitute another kind of punishment without compromising some positive impact of the traditional practice while respecting human rights.

In principle, a democratic society has some hierarchy of values that should prevail with regard to members' rights and obligations, and no one should be forced to adopt or follow a certain culture against his or her will. In this regard, cultural rights are just that—rights; they are not obligations. Community-oriented rights, on the other hand, entail duties and obligations and provide protection and support: it is not possible to enjoy one without accessing the other. The inherent contradiction between cultural rights and community rights means that, at times, group members will have to give up individual freedoms in order to receive the benefits of group cohesion. Understanding the intricacies of this trade-off should be guided by information that makes all available choices, and their consequences, clear. The provision of such information is often easier said than done, because the free circulation of such information might not be acceptable in some cultures.

Choosing to implement cultural practices might not always be possible. Regarding native language instruction, it is a relatively simple matter for a society to offer the instruction and for parents to determine whether they want their children to be taught in the language of their community or in the majority language. Regarding customary land ownership, however, it is difficult—if not impossible—for individuals to claim ownership of land when the rest of the community collectively owns this land. Conversely, recognition of customary land ownership is not possible in a system based on individual rights. The situation becomes still more complex where a people—minority or majority—attribute their legal and institutional systems to an unseen higher power, which prevents their being modified or adapted. Such views of culture often result in violent conflicts or the complete marginalization of certain groups.

Recognizing cultural rights is thus a careful balancing act, and entails intricate negotiation and in-depth understanding. Further, it is not sufficient to merely recognize traditional practices and apply them in parallel with societal laws and institutions. Bridges between the two must be built to ensure that traditional practices have a minimum level of harmonization with mainstream values and practices. As discussed in chapter 2, avoiding conflict and marginalization among societal groups requires fine-tuning, but experience shows that it is possible—many cultures actually integrate such flexibility. Marginalization is not always an issue; the example of the Amish in the United States shows that a group can live in relative isolation from mainstream society without creating conflicts. These cases are rare, however, and concern mostly religious communities supported by very specific practices.

Socioeconomic Conditions

Policies that focus on recognizing culture but do not take into account the social and economic situation of the concerned group are unlikely to succeed, particularly if they are aimed at reducing social exclusion. As discussed earlier, most indigenous people tend to be much poorer than non-indigenous people; consequently, any policies that support their inclusion need to take economic opportunity into account while recognizing their culture.

The first negative connection between a culture and its socioeconomic positioning in society is often related to prejudice and discrimination. A certain ethnicity and the culture associated with this ethnicity often trigger open or tacit discrimination.[2] Such discrimination can be manifested at school, in the labor market, while accessing basic services, as part of political participation processes, and so on. Other policies will not work if economic discrimination is not dealt with first. Many countries have thus chosen to adopt affirmative action policies as a means of breaking the cycle perpetuated by prejudice and discrimination (box 4.1).

Because many minority groups are poor, they are at risk for the poverty traps implicit in various short-term survival strategies. Encouraging a strong sense of cultural identity through public policy will not help in evading these traps and may, in some cases, actually create new traps. For example, introducing culture in the school curriculum can sometimes reinforce school segregation, which can in turn lower the quality of education and thereby set a serious poverty trap.

Poverty traps can be addressed through the creation of a safety net that allows the poor minimum economic security so they may better plan their lives. Access to such a safety net must be ensured for poor minority groups; this may entail fighting specific cultural prejudices on the part of the dominant group that can deny minorities the benefits to which they are entitled.

BOX 4.1

The Vicious Cycle of Stereotyping

Too often, prejudice and discrimination feed a vicious cycle. The inability of group members to find work, for example, reinforces stereotypes about them and gives rise to the idea that the group is unsuitable for work; this in turn pushes the group to look for other—perhaps less societally condoned—ways to survive.

A recent study by the World Bank on the employment of Roma in the Czech Republic shows that, while the unemployment figure for the Roma is low and actually quite close to that of the majority population (which was 5 percent in 2007), their level of participation in the labor force is extremely low—about 54 percent. One reason identified for this disparity is that many Roma simply believe they have no chance to find work in the formal labor market (World Bank 2008).

Cost of Multicultural Programs

The costs of recognizing cultural diversity in service delivery must be taken into account, especially in poor countries. These costs can be substantial. For example, introducing culturally sensitive policies and programs can require institutions to make several long-term changes in their outreach, communication, capacity-building, and monitoring processes. Such changes can be expensive, and their costs are often underestimated by government and development organizations. Another cost category involves the implementation of effective communication strategies addressing not only intended program beneficiaries but also aimed at helping other members of society understand why some sectors of the population receive special treatment. When value changes are involved, communication has an extremely important role to play. Outreach is necessary to make sure concerned individuals participate fully. Also, capacity building and training are often required; these costs can be extensive (box 4.2). To implement a new curriculum, for example, teachers, administrators, and school management must undergo training that helps them understand how to present the curriculum, how to avoid stigmatization, and how to avoid school segregation.

Typically, the costs associated with implementing cultural diversity policies can be high, but many are one-time, upfront costs that decrease after a few years. When these costs do decrease, multicultural policies can result in significant savings. For example, a Human Rights Watch study in

BOX 4.2

Lack of Financing Undermines Bulgarian Native Language Policy

Bulgaria recognized the right to be taught in one's native language as early as 1992. In 1999, the government passed a law that specifically required that the local language be taught at the primary and secondary school levels, if requested by a sufficient number of students. In practice, however, local governments were given no additional financing with which to do this (Gyurova 2001). Because the cost of implementing the law was never properly accounted for, the reform had little if any impact at the local level.

Guatemala estimated that $5 million—or the cost of educating 100,000 primary school students each year—was saved in the state budget by introducing bilingual education and thereby reducing repetition of classes (UNDP 2004).

Some policies might not entail upfront costs, especially when governments recognize practices that already exist or foster community-funded and -organized initiatives, such as cultural services.

The key is to identify all costs involved, explore opportunities for piggybacking and cost mitigation, and conduct a thorough cost-effectiveness assessment that takes into account both the material and nonmaterial benefits a population will gain from the policy/program.

Long-Term Investments and Strategies

Recognizing cultural diversity should not be seen as a "one-shot" measure, but rather an ongoing process that must be nurtured and adapted. As programs develop over time, institutions will need to respond to changing community needs and correct and reorient programs as necessary. The underlying plans must be strategic and flexible to ensure that the resulting programs have a long-term vision and sufficient scope to adapt and change in response to realities in the field. Introducing local languages in the curriculum and adapting the curriculum to include a minority culture may seem to be straightforward objectives, but experience shows that fine-tuning is needed along the way to improve capacity building, institutional development, and communication. Also, introducing multicultural policies may require various types of support as the minority culture adapts to its official and recognized status and the majority culture copes with the ramifications of having an additional culture legitimized. Mechanisms to manage conflict and ensure adaptation of policies and programs are generally needed.

Implementation of cultural diversity policies requires long-term investments to ensure the availability of appropriate human and other resources. Such investments might involve employing doctors from a minority group who are conversant in the local language and understand local medical practices; training enough teachers from a minority group to teach in the local language and offering incentives to entice minority students to move to the relevant areas; and hiring judges trained in customary law and able to assess cases that deal with such non-mainstream customs as witchcraft. To ensure this last, for example, means not only including this topic in the university curriculum, but also targeting and encouraging students with the requisite understanding and sensitivity to enroll in the field.

Policy makers must understand that the demand for recognizing cultural practices can vary over time. Demand for studying in a minority language can suddenly increase or decrease in response to changing situations. This does not mean that the relationship between people and their culture is erratic, but rather that external circumstances play a role in influencing the demand for individuated culture.

Evaluation

Information is limited on how policies and programs that support cultural diversity have affected communities. There is more analysis of education than of other sectors, but that research focuses mostly on the impact of introducing local languages and teaching in native languages. Overall, the findings of these assessments are positive, with the caveats that investments in training and institution building are often underestimated, and the quality of teaching remains a real issue for languages that are very specific or marginalized. In the area of health care, the WHO has conducted some solid case studies on the impact of traditional medicine and how health services have been adapted to fit the cultural context, but these are limited to just a few regions. On the topics of customary law, local governance, and cultural services, assessments are extremely limited and consist mostly of descriptive case studies. Furthermore, many assessments are not comparable and are based on small individual communities.

More must be done in evaluating the impact of policies and programs on overall sectoral outcomes, social cohesion, and social inclusion. Collecting best practices and deriving a better understanding of the relevant political, economic, and institutional issues are critical in moving forward.

Cost-effectiveness analysis is vital; but this entails a number of challenges. The costs of putting cultural diversity policies related to service delivery into effect vary widely, based on whether the involved population is poor, how well it is integrated in mainstream society, the capacity and institutional development of the local civil society, and so on. For example, teaching Hungarian to Hungarian minorities in Romania does not incur the same costs as teaching in the Roma language. There are many teachers of Hungarian descent, and Hungary has textbooks and established methodologies that can be made available free of charge to Hungarian communities in other countries. Teaching in the Roma language, on the other hand, requires teacher training, new textbooks, identification of appropriate pedagogical methods, implementation of a communication campaign aimed at helping parents understand the benefits of such education for their children, development of strategies to avoid discrimination toward children who study the Roma language in school, and so on. Similarly, having doctors of Mayan origin work in Mayan areas in Mexico is much more difficult and costly than having Maori doctors work in Maori areas in New Zealand. There are many Maori doctors, and the living conditions of the involved areas are of sufficient quality to attract many of them to the assignment. Mexico, on the other hand, has very few Mayan doctors. Training them is expensive, as is creating the basic infrastructure to make Mayan areas attractive to external professionals. This stark differentiation in initial conditions is only one example of the difficulty of carrying out cost-effectiveness comparisons among countries.

Finally, politics can have a significant impact on cost-efficiency. This is true for most types of projects, but cultural issues tend to be much more politicized because of their link to identity issues. More analysis is needed, preferably on the impact policies and programs have had on communities in Ghana, South Africa, and Uganda in Africa; Malaysia, the Philippines, Thailand, and Vietnam in Asia; Bulgaria, Hungary, and Romania in Eastern Europe; Bolivia, Guatemala, and Mexico in Latin America; and Australia, New Zealand, Papua New Guinea, and many of the smaller Pacific islands in Oceania—all of which have tried to implement multicultural policies and programs for a relatively long period of time. Such an analysis should include a mix of political and institutional data with outcome measurements wherever possible. Communities where such policies have not yet been introduced can be used as control groups. This kind of comprehensive analysis would offer a better understanding of the practical issues involved in the implementation of multicultural policies. Sectoral analysis should also be increased in the fields of education, health care, customary law, and customary dispute resolution mechanisms.

Notes

1. Some countries have refused to take such a step, arguing that it would alter the very nature of the state itself. France, for instance, sees recognition of cultural diversity in the public sphere as a threat to the Republican principle of equality. For this reason, France has not ratified a number of important treaties related to teaching minority languages in public schools.
2. According to the Minorities at Risk data set created by researchers at the University of Maryland's Center for International Development and Conflict Management, some 750 million people in the world today belong to groups that face socioeconomic discrimination or disadvantage (or both) as a result of their cultural identity; for about 68 million of these people, this treatment is the result of directly discriminatory government policies.

CHAPTER 5

Adapting Services to a Diverse Society

Since the late 1980s, policies and programs that support cultural diversity have acquired a new visibility in the international arena. The end of the Cold War witnessed the rise of a new global society that many fear threatens to homogenize the world. As a result, culture has become increasingly important for identity formation around the world. There is also increasing evidence that recognizing at least some level of cultural diversity can reduce conflict and increase collective agency. Moreover, recognizing cultural diversity and fighting poverty are seen as complementary activities: inequality continues to be strongly correlated with ethnic and cultural differences, and it is now quite clear that recognizing cultural differences can reduce inequality.

The growing demand to recognize cultural diversity raises a number of important issues for countries around the world. Policies supporting cultural diversity can at times be at odds with the principle of homogenous citizenship that promises similar rights and obligations for all. With some variation, this principle has been one of the pillars of the European and North American nation-state since the French and American revolutions of the 18th century. Recognizing cultural diversity therefore often requires important changes in the legal and institutional frameworks of many countries as well as in the political culture. In numerous countries, international recognition of the importance of multicultural policies is moving faster than their actual implementation, driven by the UN, the Council of Europe, the Organization of American States, and various human rights organizations and other multilateral institutions.

A critical component of multicultural policies is making sure that basic services are adapted to fit the practices and values of groups that comprise a nation. Such policies and programs need to be anchored to local realities

75

and institutions, such as the school, the health center, the local government and its administrative organization, and festivals and other cultural events. All of these entities and activities are important in both identity building and collective agency. But adapting services to the cultural reality of various groups must be undertaken with the overall objective of improving social cohesion, lest further social tension and exclusion be created.

Many countries have experimented with designing policies that support cultural diversity. Early evidence indicates that the majority of these efforts have positively affected the societies in which they've been instituted. There have been places in which multicultural policies have negatively affected communities, but these have most often been the result of poor planning or execution. For example, where policies have lacked the proper means, support, training, funding, or attention, they have contributed to the exclusion of some social groups, such as women or youth.

Despite the attention given to cultural diversity in recent years, thorough analysis regarding the impact of cultural diversity policies is lacking. Moreover, because many efforts are new and ongoing, their long-term social impacts remain to be seen. Quantitative assessments are usually limited to the field of bilingual education and learning in the native language; most of the assessments in other areas are still qualitative or quantitative only with regard to small and limited samples. The international development community should strive to conduct systematic assessments and analyses of policies and programs that support cultural diversity in service delivery.

Some impacts have been identified. Broad evidence indicates that teaching the curriculum in local languages and incorporating various cultures into curricular materials on history, geography, and art reduce tensions, improve social integration, and enrich the cognitive performance of children in their lifelong educational endeavors. However, these outcomes result only when a program is properly outfitted with teacher training, teacher assistants, community outreach, and communication. In the health care sector, the recognition of cultural diversity has been shown to have a positive effect on the health of ethnically diverse populations. The experiences to date with service delivery through local governance systems underscore the importance of ensuring full participation of diverse ethnic communities but raise issues about protecting individual rights and supporting participation of all members of a community. In all of these areas, more analysis is needed; such efforts should be accompanied by the collection and description of best practices.

Experience clearly shows that governments should not dictate multicultural policies in a top-down manner, but should instead foster an environment where local and majority cultures can interact peacefully and productively. It is essential to respect the diversity of, and even the contradictions in, human aspirations. Recognizing local cultures in public policy and service delivery is an ongoing process, not a single one-time action. Governments must avoid taking a piecemeal approach to the promotion of cultural diversity and be prepared to meet the additional requirements of capacity building and institutional development.

As globalization progresses, it is less expected that all citizens be strongly integrated into a nation-state and adopt a homogeneous central culture. Refusing to acknowledge this trend only delays the process of social integration, which further reduces social cohesion. In a world where change is often viewed as a source of anxiety instead of an opportunity, it can help to admit our cultural differences. As long as some of a society's core values can be respected and preserved, admitting cultural differences helps people find a meaningful identity while remaining, or becoming, engaged citizens. Policies that recognize cultural diversity should therefore be seen as important components of the social response to globalization, and ultimately be integrated into new social policies in countries around the world.

What Is Cultural Identity?

The concept of *identity* as used by psychologists describes a sense of being and belonging to a community that is essential in managing interactions with others. The concept of *culture* is generally applied by anthropologists to communities or societies—that is, to the "collective" dimension of human beings. *Cultural identity* lies at the intersection of these terms, as both a psychological and social construct.

Identity is a central constitutive element in the psychology of a human being. It is identity that makes us feel that we are an agent of our own development, and identity that helps us see ourselves both as an individual human being with a unique existence and, at the same time, as an integral part of a collective or societal body. The concept thus has a strong "existential" quality and is central to agency, which is the ability to act in society, and especially in one's own life. People cannot operate normally in society without an identity, or with a weakened one. George Mead, one of the fathers of social psychology, describes identity as the integration of social norms expressed in the "self," and the spontaneous and personal expressed in the term "I" (Mead 1934). Identity therefore varies by society and culture, depending on the space available for individual autonomy. Modernity is sometimes described as the evolution of identity from collective and group-based to more individual and autonomous (Morin 2004).

Identity is made up of several components. The first component is linked to a sense of being in existence, which in turns makes one feel that life is worth living. Psychiatrist Eric Erikson describes identity in his 1968 book *Identity, Youth and Crisis* as "something that comes upon you as a recognition" (p. 20). This is primordial identity, the type of existential experience described by philosophers such as Jean Paul Sartre and Albert Camus.

But identity is also linked to a sense of sameness and differentiation. This is the important collective dimension of identity. People reinforce their sense of being by identifying with some and differentiating from others. The individual human being in society needs to look for similarities and differences with the "other." This means that identity cannot exist without a consciousness of the other and of the vision the other has of oneself (Levinas 1981). The sense of being can be understood by the "me" and the "you"—that is, by one's recognition *of* the other and one's recognition *by* the other (Ricoeur 1994). Recognition is thus an essential ingredient in the experience of being a personal and social entity. People also need to adopt the characteristics that will allow them to be accepted by others and to have a sense of sameness as well as of difference.

The way identity is built varies by society. In societies in which the individual has very little autonomy, it is more important to preserve the group identity. The collective (expressed through rituals and rigid sets of rules) tends to dictate to the individual his or her identity, and therefore the similarities with and differences from other members of the same group. In societies that value more autonomy, the individual has more choices for establishing an identity independent of the group. However, along with choice comes an increased anxiety and strong existential fear of being responsible for deciding one's identity, which is often considered one of the more fragile aspects of the human being in modern societies.

The formation of identity corresponds strongly to age (Erikson 1968). Humans relate to their identities differently at various points in their life. An infant experiences a sense of being that is undifferentiated from the surrounding world; this sense of being is strongly embedded in the child's physical and emotional relationship with its mother and is central to the development of its psychology. A feeling of differentiation from the surrounding world begins to appear between the ages of one and three; at this point, relations are established by the child with the father and with other members of the child's family and group. The child becomes aware of a separation between "I" and the rest of the world, and begins to assume various identities. From the ages of three to seven, the child starts to recognize multiple identities. He or she becomes conscious of various social roles and integrates a sense of belonging to various groups. This is the stage at which culture becomes directly influential.

Adolescence is a time of very strong collective identification, when the young person leaves a system of reference still very much linked to his or her family and others and assumes a social autonomy independent from those with whom he or she is close. Adolescence is recognized in all cultures as a central life stage when an individual acquires autonomy. In many traditions, this period is marked by elaborate rites of passage. Identity continues to change during adult life, but in a less dramatic fashion than during youth and adolescence.

Identity formation is situated at the juncture of the real and the imagined. Each individual and group is part of a tangible reality, but this reality is structured and plays as an identity through a mental construct built as a synthesis between individual and collective imagery (Lévi-Strauss 1952). For instance, a flag is a piece of textile, but it creates a sense of national identity—and it is what the flag evokes in someone that is important for identity. The mental representation constitutes an interpretative and ethical framework for the individual which will dictate and justify his or her actions in society.

Collective identity is important in cultures that promote both individual autonomy and group cohesion. Collective identity has many positive elements in terms of creating group cohesion, supporting internal solidarity, and establishing rules that aid in social transactions, but it can also be a source of conservatism, and a means of maintaining cultural barriers that hinder the progress of the group as a whole and the root of violent conflict between groups. In and of itself, however, collective identity is neither negative nor positive, but a societal characteristic that requires acknowledgment rather than judgment.

African Union. 2005. "Plan of Action of the Decade of Traditional Medicine (2001–2010)." CAMH/15. Addis Ababa: African Union.

Andreescu, Viviana. 2005. "Cultural Diversity and Service Delivery." Report prepared for the World Bank study, *Cultural Diversity and Delivery of Services: A Major Challenge for Social Cohesion*. Washington, DC: World Bank.

Appadurai, Arjun. 1966. *Modernity at Large, Cultural Dimension of Globalization*. Minneapolis: University of Minnesota Press.

Banks, James A. 2001. "Multicultural Education: Historical Development, Dimensions and Practice." In James A. Banks and Cherry A. McGee Banks, eds., *Handbook of Research on Multicultural Education*. San Francisco: Jossey-Bass.

Basian J. W. 1982. "Exchange between Andean and Western Medicine." *Social Science and Medicine* 16(7).

Benmayor, Rina, and Andor Skotnes, eds. 2005. *Migration and Identity*. Edison, NJ: Transaction Publishers.

Beaton, N. 1994. "Aboriginal Health and New Curriculum for Rural Doctors." *Medical Journal of Australia* 160(4).

Bhopal, Raj. 2007. *Ethnicity, Race and Health in a Multicultural Environment: Foundations for Better Epidemiology, Public Health, and Health Care*. Oxford, UK: Oxford University Press.

Bourdieu, Pierre. 1982. *Ce que parler veut dire, l'économie des échanges linguistiques*. Paris: Editions Fayard.

———. 2001. *Langage et pouvoir symbolique*. Paris: Editions du Seuil.

Brettell, Caroline. *Anthropology and Migration: Essays on Transnationalism, Ethnicity, and Identity*. Lanham, MD: AltaMira Press.

Capotorti, Francesco. 1991. *Study on the Rights of Persons Belonging to Ethnic, Religious and Linguistic Minorities*. Geneva: United Nations Center for Human Rights.

Cardona, Ricardo Grisales. 2005. "Diversidad cultural y gobernabilidad." Report prepared for the World Bank study, *Cultural Diversity and Delivery of Services: A Major Challenge for Social Cohesion*. Washington, DC: World Bank.

Care, Jennifer Corrin. 1999. "Conflict between Customary Law and Human Rights in the South Pacific." Paper presented at the Commonwealth Law Conference, Kuala Lumpur, September 1999.

Castells, Manuel. 1997. *The Power of Identity*. Oxford: Blackwell Publishers.

CIE (Center for International Economics). 2002. *Vietnam Poverty Analysis*. Canberra: CIE.

Coombe, Rosemary. 2005. "Cultural Rights and Intellectual Property Debate." *Human Rights Dialogue* 2(12).

Cott, Lee Van. 2000. *The Friendly Liquidation of the Past: The Politics of Diversity in Latin America*. Pittsburgh, PA: University of Pittsburgh Press.

CSCE (Conference on Security and Co-operation in Europe). 1990. "Document of the Copenhagen Meeting of the Conference on the Human Dimension of the CSCE." Vienna: CSCE.

Dani, Anis, and Arjan de Haan, eds. 2008. *Inclusive States: Social Policy and Structural Inequalities*. Washington, DC: World Bank.

Dasgupta, Parha, and Ismail Serageldin. 1999. *Social Capital: A Multifaceted Perspective*. Washington, DC: World Bank.

Davis, Shelton. 2004. "The Mayan Movement and National Culture in Guatemala." In Vijayendra Rao and Michael Walton, eds., *Culture and Public Action*. Stanford, CA: Stanford University Press.

De Ferrenti, David, Guillermo Perry, Francisco Ferreira, and Michael Walton. 2004. *Inequality in Latin America: Breaking with History*. Washington, DC: World Bank.

Deshingar, Priya, and Sven Grimm. 2005. "Internal Migration and Development: A Global Perspective." Research Series No. 19. Geneva: Institute of Medicine.

De Soto, H., P. Gordon, I. Gedeshi, and Z. Sinoimeri. 2002. "Poverty in Albania: A Qualitative Assessment." Technical Paper No. 520. Washington, DC: World Bank.

Diekhoff, Alain. 2002. *La nation dans tous ses états: Les identités nationales en mouvement*. Paris: Flammarion.

Douglas, Mary. 2004. "Traditional Culture, Let's Hear No More About It." In Michael Walton and Vijayendra Rao, eds., *Culture and Public Action*. Washington, DC: World Bank.

Dubar, Claude. 2000. *La crise des identités. La interprétation d'une mutation*. Paris: Presses Universitaires de France.

Dudwick, N., E. Gomart, A. Marc, and K. Kuehnast, eds. 2003. *When Things Fall Apart: Qualitative Studies of Poverty in the Former Soviet Union*. Washington, DC: World Bank.

Dutcher, N., and G. K. Tucker. 1997. *The Use of First and Second Languages in Education: A Review of Educational Experience*. Washington, DC: World Bank.

Erikson, Erik. 1968. *Identity: Youth and Crisis*. New York: Norton.

Garkawe, Sam. 1995. "The Impact of the Doctrine of Cultural Relativism on the Australian Legal System." *Murdoch University Electronic Journal of Law* 2(1).

Ghai, Yash. 1998. "Decentralization and the Accommodation of Ethnic Diversity." In Crawford Young, ed., *Ethnic Diversity and Public Policy: A Comparative Inquiry*. London: Macmillan.

Gibbal, Jean-Marie. 1984. *Guérisseurs et magiciens du Sahel.* Paris: Editions A. M. Metailie.

Giddens, Anthony. 1990. *The Consequences of Modernity.* Stanford, CA: Stanford University Press.

Government of New South Wales. 2006. "Cultural Planning Guidelines for Local Government." Sydney: Ministry of the Arts and Ministry of Department of Local Governments.

Guggenheim, Scott, Tatag Wiranto, Yogana Prasta, and Susan Wong. 2004. "Indonesia's Kecamatan Development Program: A Large-Scale Use of Community Development to Reduce Poverty." Working Paper 30779. Washington, DC: World Bank.

Greaney, Vincent. 2006. "Textbooks, Respect for Diversity, and Social Cohesion." In Eluned Roberts-Schweitzer, Vincent Greaney, and Krezentia Duer, eds., *Promoting Social Cohesion through Education: Case Studies and Tools for Using Textbooks.* Washington DC: World Bank.

Guewardena, D., and D. Van de Walle. 2000. "Sources of Ethnic Inequality in Viet Nam." *Journal of Development Economics* 65: 177–207.

Gyurova, Elena. 2001. "Emerging Multi-Ethnic Policies in Bulgaria: A Central-Local Perspective." In Anna-Mária Bíró and Petra Kovács, eds., *Diversity in Action: Local Public Management of Multi-Ethnic Communities in Central and Eastern Europe.* Budapest: Local Government and Public Service Reform Initiative.

Hall, Gillette, and Harry Patrinos, eds. 2005. *Indigenous Peoples, Poverty and Human Development in Latin America: 1994–2004.* Washington, DC: World Bank.

———. 2009. *Indigenous Peoples, Poverty and Development.* Washington, DC: World Bank.

Hermanine, Costanza. 2005. "Revue de littérature sur la diversité culturelle et les services de base." Report prepared for the World Bank study, *Cultural Diversity and Delivery of Services: A Major Challenge for Social Cohesion.* Washington, DC: World Bank.

Hirschman, Albert O. 1970. *Exit, Voice and Loyalty: Responses to Decline in Firms, Organizations and States.* Cambridge, MA: Harvard University Press.

Hopenhayn, Marin. 2008 "Recognition and Distribution: Equity and Justice for Discriminated Groups in Latin America." In Anis Dani and Arjan de Haan, eds., *Inclusive States: Social Policy and Structural Inequalities.* Washington, DC: World Bank.

Jaffrelot, Christophe. 2005. *La démocratie par la caste: Histoire d'une mutation socio-politique 1885–2005.* Paris: Fayard.

Jenkins, Richard. 2008. *Social Identity.* London: Taylor & Francis.

Kepel, Gilles. 1991. *La revanche de Dieu, Chrétiens, Juifs et Musulmans à la reconquête du monde.* Paris: Editions du Seuil.

King, Linda, and Sabine Schielmann. 2004. "The Challenge of Indigenous Education: Practice and Perspectives." Paris: United Nations Educational, Scientific and Cultural Organization.

Kymlicka, Will. 1995. *Multicultural Citizenship*. Oxford: Oxford University Press.

———. 2003. "Culturally Responsive Policies." Paper prepared for the 2004 United Nations Development Programme *Human Development Report*. New York: United Nations Development Programme.

———. 2007. *Multicultural Odysseys: Navigating the New International Politics of Diversity*. Oxford: Oxford University Press.

Kymlicka, Will, and François Grin. 2003. "Assessing the Politics of Diversity in Transition Countries." In Farimah Daftary and François Grin, eds., *Nation-Building, Ethnicity and Language Politics in Transition*. Budapest: Central European University.

Leveau, Rémy, Withol de Wenden, and Khadija Mohsen-Finan. 2003. "De la citoyenneté locale." Paris: Institut Français des Relations Internationales.

Lévi-Strauss, Claude. 1952. *Race et histoire*. Paris: Folio.

Levinas, Emmanuel. 1981. *Otherwise Than Being or Beyond Essence*. New York: Springer.

Liegois, Jean Pierre. 2007. *Les Roms en Europe*. Strasbourg, France: Conseil de l'Europe.

Litteral, Robert. 2004. "Vernacular Education in Papua Guinea." Background paper prepared for the 2005 *Education for All Global Monitoring Report*." 2005/ED/EFA/MRT/PI/30. Paris: United Nations Educational, Scientific and Cultural Organization.

Loury, Glenn C. 2001. *The Anatomy of Racial Inequality*. Cambridge, MA: Harvard University Press.

Luyx, Aurolyn. 1999. *The Citizen Factory Schooling and Cultural Production in Bolivia*. New York: State University of New York Press.

Narayan, Deepa, and Patti Petesch. 2002. *Voices of the Poor: From Many Lands*. New York: Oxford University Press.

Marc, Alexandre. 2008. "Taking Culture into Account in the Delivery of Health and Education Services." In Anis Dani and Arjan de Haan, eds., *Inclusive States: Social Policy and Structural Inequalities*. Washington, DC: World Bank.

Mead, George Herbert. 1934. *Mind, Self, and Society: From the Perspective of a Social Behaviorist*. Chicago: University of Chicago Press.

Mehotra, S. 1998. "Education for All: Policy Lessons from High Achieving Countries." UNICEF Staff Working Paper. New York: United Nations Children's Fund.

Ministerio de Salud Pública y Asistencia Social. 2004. "Programas Nacional Medicina Popular, Tradicional y Alternativa: Conociendo la medicina Maya en Guatemala." Guatemala City: Modulo de Sensibilización.

Moodley, Kogila A. 2001. "Multicultural Education in Canada: Historical Development and Current Status." In James A. Banks and Cherry A. McGee Banks, eds., *Handbook of Research on Multicultural Education*. San Francisco: Jossey-Bass.

Morales, Lourdes. 2005. "Practicas Electorales en Totontepec Villa de Morelos." Report prepared for the Centre d'Études et de Recherches International. Paris.

Morin, Edgar. 2004. *Le paradigme perdu: La nature humaine*. Paris: Editions du Seuil.

North, Douglass C. 1990. *Institutions, Institutional Change and Economic Performance*. Cambridge, UK: Cambridge University Press.

Open Society Institute. 2006. "Equality for Roma in Europe: A Roadmap for Action." New York: Open Society Institute.

Pieterse, Jan Nederveen. 2004. *Globalization and Culture, Global Mélange*. Lanham, MD: Rowman & Littlefield.

Ping, Huang, and Zhan Shahua. 2005. "Internal Migration in China: Linking It to Development." Paper prepared for the regional conference on Migration and Development in Asia. Lanzhou.

Posey, Darell, and Graham Dutfield. 1996. *Beyond Cultural Property: Towards Traditional Rights for Indigenous Peoples and Local Communities*. Ottawa: International Development Research Center.

Ratha, Dilip, and William Shaw. 2007. "South-South Migration and Remittances." Washington, DC: World Bank.

Recondo, David. 2007. "From Acclamation to Secret Ballot: The Hybridisation of Voting Procedures in Mexican-Indian Communities." In Romain Bertrand, Jean-Louis Briquet, and Peter Pels, eds., *Cultures of Voting: The Hidden History of the Secret Ballot*, pp. 156–79. London: CERI-Hurst.

Ricoeur, Paul. 1994. *Oneself as Another*. Chicago: University of Chicago Press.

Ringold, Dena. 2005. "Accounting for Diversity: Policy Design and Maori Development in Aotearoa New Zealand." Report prepared for the Ian Axford (New Zealand) Fellowship in Public Policy.

Ringold, Dena A., Mitchell Orenstein, and Erika Williams. 2003. *Roma in an Expanding Europe: Breaking the Poverty Cycle*. Washington, DC: World Bank.

Roma Education Fund. 2007. "The Case for Integrated Education." *A School for All* 1 (December).

Rossell, Christine H., D. J. Armor, and H. J. Walberg. 2002. *School Desegregation in the 21st Century*. Westport, CT: Praeger Publishers.

Sabbagh, Daniel. 2003. "Affirmative Action Policies: An International Perspective." Background paper for *Human Development Report* 2004. New York: United Nations Development Programme.

Sen, Amartya. 1999. *Development as Freedom*. New York: Oxford University Press.

———. 2009. *The Idea of Justice*. London: Allan Lane.

Sheineson, Andrew. 2009. "China's Internal Migrants." Council on Foreign Relations *Backgrounder*. www.cfr.org/publication/12943/.

Sieder, Rachel, ed. 2002. *Multiculturalism in Latin America: Indigenous Rights Diversity and Democracy.* London: Macmillan.

Smith, Alana. 2006. "Education for Diversity: Investing in Systemic Change through Curriculum, Textbooks, and Teachers." In Eluned Roberts-Schweitzer, Vincent Greaney, and Krezentia Duer, eds., *Promoting Social Cohesion through Education: Case Studies and Tools for Using Textbooks.* Washington DC: World Bank.

Stephens, C., C. Nettleton, J. Porter, R. Willis, and S. Clark. 2005. "Indigenous People's Health—Why Are They Behind Everyone, Everywhere?" *Lancet* 366(9479): 10–13.

Taylor, Charles. 1994. *Multiculturalism: Examining the Politics of Recognition.* Princeton, NJ: Princeton University Press.

Thiesse, Anne-Marie. 1999. *La création des identités nationales, Europe XVIII-XX siècle.* Paris: Editions du Seuil.

Thomberry, Patrick. 2001. "An Unfinished Agenda." In Anna-Mária Bíró and Petra Kovács, eds., *Diversity in Action, Local Public Management of Multi-Ethnic Communities in Central and Eastern Europe.* Budapest: Open Society Institute.

Thual, François. 1995. *Les conflits identitaires.* Paris: Editions Elipses.

Tomlinson, John. 1999. *Globalization and Culture.* Chicago: University of Chicago Press.

Touraine, Alain. 2005. *Un nouveau paradigme pour comprendre le monde d'aujourd'hui.* Paris: Fayard.

Tripp, Aili Mari. 2004. "Women's Movements, Customary Law and Land Rights in Africa: The Case of Uganda." *African Studies Quarterly* 7(4).

United Nations Department of Economic and Social Affairs. 2009 *International Migration Report 2006.* New York: United Nations.

United Nations General Assembly. 1992. "Declaration on the Rights of Persons Belonging to National or Ethnic, Religious and Linguistic Minorities." A/RES/47/135. New York: United Nations.

UNDP (United Nations Development Programme). 2004. *Human Development Report: Cultural Liberty in Today's Diverse World.* New York: UNDP.

UNESCO (United Nations Educational, Scientific and Cultural Organization). 2002. "Universal Declaration on Cultural Identity." Paris: UNESCO.

———. 2003. "Education in a Multilingual World." Position paper. Paris: United Nations Educational, Scientific and Cultural Organization.

Waters, F. William. 2007. "The Contribution of Local Organizations to Improved Service Delivery in Bolivia." Paper prepared for the World Bank Social Protection Advisory Services to the Government of Bolivia. Washington, DC: World Bank.

Webster, Yehudi O. 1997. *Against the Multicultural Agenda: A Critical Thinking Alternative.* Westport, CT: Praeger Publishers.

WHO (World Health Organization). 2002. *WHO Traditional Medicine Strategy, 2002–2005.* Geneva: WHO.

Wieviorka, Michel. 1993. *La Démocratie à l'épreuve: Nationalisme, populisme, ethnicité.* Paris: Editions La Découverte.

Winnicott, D. W. 1992. *The Family and Individual Development.* London: Routledge.

World Bank. 2004. "Village Justice in Indonesia: Case Studies on Access to Justice, Village Democracy and Governance." Social Development Paper No. 62. Washington, DC: World Bank.

———. 2005. "Guatemala Public Expenditure Review." Washington, DC: World Bank.

———. 2008. *Czech Republic: Improving Employment Chances of the Roma.* Report No. 46120 CZ. Washington, DC: World Bank.

———. 2009. "Emergency Project Paper on a Proposed Additional Grant to the Islamic Republic of Afghanistan Second Emergency National Solidarity Project." Report No. 48224-AF. Washington, DC: World Bank.

Yoder, P. S. 1982. "Biomedical and Ethnomedical Practice in Rural Zaire: Contrasts and Complements." *Social Science and Medicine* 16(21): 1851–57.

Young, Crawford, ed. 1998. *Ethnic Diversity and Public Policy: A Comparative Inquiry.* London: Macmillan.

Boxes are indicated by an italic b.

A

affirmative action, 21, 69
Afghanistan, 52
Africa
    cultural norms and entrepreneurism in, 27
    education in, 32, 33, 54n1
    HIV/AIDS in, 43–44
    language policies and instruction in, 33, 54n1
    polygamy, rise in, 28
    traditional medicine in, 43–44
African Americans, 18, 21
African Regional Strategy on Traditional Medicine, 44
African Union, 44
agency, concept of, 16, 17b, 25–26
AIDS/HIV, 43–44
Albania, 9, 38b, 48, 50, 51b, 62, 73
American Indians
    Latin American. *See under* Latin America
    North American, 47, 49
Amish, 69
appropriation, cultural, 47
Arab world
    effects of cultural diversity in, 7
    France, Islam in, 10
    international migration to Gulf countries, 8
    Islamist groups, 52
    Israel, Jews and Arabs in, 16, 20
    youth subculture in North Africa, 12
Argentina, 8, 11
arts, traditional, 47

Asia
    education, multicultural, 32
    effects of cultural diversity in, 7
    poverty of ethnic minorities in, 24
    traditional medicine in, 43
assimilation
    resistance to, 11
    social inclusion, assimilationist approach to, 16, 74n1
Australia, 11, 36, 42, 48, 73

B

Bamilekes, 23b
Basque immigration to Argentina, 11
Be baskets, 47
Belgium, 15
Bhutan, 43
bilingual education, 34, 36, 38, 39, 40b, 71
blood feuds, 51b
Bolivia, 8, 9, 19, 22, 39, 50, 73
Botswana, 54n1
Bourdieu, Pierre, 25–26
Bulgaria, 23, 38, 71b, 73
Burkina Faso, 8, 47
Burma. *See* Myanmar

C

Cameroon, 23b
Camus, Albert, 79
Canada, 4, 11, 14, 32, 57
cargo, sistema de (Latin America), 51
caste systems, 20, 21, 22, 27, 29, 50, 54, 65
Ceddo (film), 28n1
China, 8, 10, 24, 33, 43, 46
Chinese in Malaysia, 23b

citizenship
balance between citizens' rights and
cultural rights, 67–69
multicultural, concept of, 14–17
collective and individual identity, 58–59,
80, 81
Colombia, 8, 14, 16, 19
communitarian approach to social inclusion, 16
community and individual identity, 58–59,
80, 81
community initiatives, supporting, 48–49
community rights, 68
conflict reduction mechanisms, 26
Convention 169 Concerning Indigenous
and Tribal Peoples in Independent
Countries (ILO), 13b
corporate decentralization, 19–20
costs of multicultural programs, 70–71,
71b, 73
Côte d'Ivoire, 8, 9–10
crafts, traditional, 47, 49
cultural appropriation, 47
cultural competence, concept of, 40–41
cultural diversity, 1–5, 75–77
definitions pertinent to, 1–4, 2b
in education, 5, 31–39, 32b, 34b, 36b,
38b, 63, 76
in health care, 5, 40–46, 42b, 45b, 72
literature review, 4, 46–47
local governments, service delivery by, 1,
4–5, 31–55. See also local governments and cultural diversity
mobility and. See mobility and cultural
diversity
national government management of, 4,
7–29. See also national public policy
and cultural diversity
policies for service delivery and, 5,
57–74. See also policies supporting
cultural diversity in service delivery
risks of, 26–28, 51b
cultural identity, defined, 79–81
cultural minorities, defined, 10b. See also
minority populations
cultural rights
citizens' rights and, 67–69
government management of cultural
diversity and, 18
international recognition of, 12–14, 13b

laws and regulations, culturally specific
exceptions to, 20
profits from cultural tourism, ownership
of, 47, 48–49
reduction of cultural exclusion, public
policy aimed at, 22
cultural services in culturally diverse societies, 5, 46–49
cultural tourism, 46–49
culture, defined, 2b
Czech Republic, 36b, 70b

D

Decade of African Traditional Medicine
(2001–10), 44
decentralization, 19–20, 65–66
Declaration on Race and Racial Prejudice,
13b
Democratic Peoples' Republic of Korea, 14
design of policies. See policies supporting
cultural diversity in service delivery
discrimination, public policy combating,
20–22
Douglas, Mary, 2b

E

Eastern and Central Europe. See also specific countries
education, multicultural, 32
language policies in, 33, 38, 39, 40b
Roma of. See Roma
economics of multicultural programs,
70–71, 71b, 73
Ecuador, 8, 9, 14, 19
education in culturally diverse societies, 5,
31–39, 32b, 34b, 36b, 38b, 63, 76
Egypt, Arab Republic of, 20
elders, councils of, 50–52, 51b
emigration. See mobility and cultural
diversity
employment policies, 63, 69, 70b
Erikson, Erik, 79
Eritrea, 19, 54n1
Ethiopia, 19, 53, 54n1
ethnic groups, defined, 10b
European Charter for Regional or Minority Languages, 64
European Union (EU), 8, 14, 40b, 64, 75
evaluation processes for cultural diversity
policies, 72–74

F

festivals, celebrating, 46, 47, 50
financing multicultural programs, 70–71,
71*b*, 73
fis (Albania), 50, 51*b*
fokonolona (Madagascar), 50
France, 10, 12, 16, 74n1
French Revolution, 15, 16

G

Galician immigration to Argentina, 11
gender issues
avoiding exclusion of women, 76
cultural norms leading to gender discrimination, 27
health care, 42
Mauritania, female autonomy in, 29n10
polygamy, 27, 28
stakeholder participation, importance
of, 67
tontines, 29n8
traditional local governance mechanisms
and, 51–52, 51*b*
German minorities of Eastern and Central
Europe, 39
Ghai, Yash, 19
Ghana, 19, 43, 53, 73
globalization
cultural change accelerated by, 58
cultural diversity promoted by, 77
link between territory and culture weakened by, 10–11
government management of cultural
diversity. *See* local government and
cultural diversity; national public
policy and cultural diversity
Grin, François, 33
Guatemala, 9, 24, 48, 61, 63, 65, 66, 71, 73
Gulf countries, international migration to, 8

H

habitus, 26
La Haine (film), 12
health care in culturally diverse societies, 5,
40–46, 42*b*, 45*b*, 72
HIV/AIDS, 43–44
Hopi, 49
Human Development Report (UNDP,
2004), 1, 13, 18, 20
human rights and minority/ethnic rights, 15

Hungary and ethnic Hungarians, 14, 23*b*,
36, 38, 39, 40*b*, 61, 65, 73
hybridization, defined, 2*b*

I

Iceland, 14
identity
changing models of, 3–4
community/collective versus individual,
58–59, 80, 81
cultural identity, defined, 79–81
self-identification, changing models of,
3–4
ILO (International Labour Organization),
Convention 169 Concerning Indigenous and Tribal Peoples in Independent Countries, 13*b*
immigration. *See* mobility and cultural
diversity
implementation of policies. *See* policies
supporting cultural diversity in service
delivery
India, 8, 19, 20, 21–22, 27, 29n5, 43, 47,
65
Indians, Latin American. *See under* Latin
America
Indians, North American, 47, 49
indigenous peoples. *See also* specific
peoples, e.g., Masai
defined, 10*b*
health care for, 40
ILO Convention 169, 13*b*
in Latin America. *See under* Latin
America
Native Americans (North America), 47,
49
poverty, living in, 23–24
indirect rule tradition, 53
individuation and cultural diversity, 3,
58–59
Indonesia, 8, 19, 50, 52
inequality
assimilation, resistance to, 11
discrimination, public policy combating,
20–22
marginalization of cultural groups, 69
mobility due to, 9
poverty targeting, 23–25, 23*b*
recognition of specific cultural rights to
combat, 18

socioeconomic conditions of cultural groups, 69, 74n2
integrated multisectoral approach to cultural policies, 62–63
integrationist approach to social inclusion, 16
International Convention on the Elimination of All Forms of Racial Discrimination, 13b
International Covenant on Civil and Political Rights, 12, 28n2
International Covenant on Economic, Social and Cultural Rights, 12
International Declaration on the Rights of Persons Belonging to National or Ethnic, Religious or Linguistic Minorities, 13b
International Labour Organization (ILO), Convention 169 Concerning Indigenous and Tribal Peoples in Independent Countries, 13b
international migration, 8
international recognition of cultural rights, 12–14, 13b, 64, 75
Irish immigration to United States, 11
Islamist groups of the Middle East, 52. See also Arab world; religion
Israel, 16, 20
Italian immigration to Argentina, 11

J

Jews and Judaism, 16, 20

K

Kanun (Albania), 51b
Kassovitz, Mathieu, 12
Kenya, 19, 47, 48
Korea, Democratic Peoples' Republic of, 14
Korea, Republic of, 14
kosher requirements, 20
Kosovo, 38b
Kymlicka, Will, 3, 17, 33

L

labor market policies, 63, 69, 70b
land ownership, 20–21, 68
language
European Charter for Regional or Minority Languages, 64
health care and, 41
native language/bilingual instruction,

33–34, 34b, 36–39, 40b, 68, 71b, 72, 73
Latin America
education in, 32, 36
effects of cultural diversity in, 7
indigenous peoples of
migration in, 9
policies regarding, 61, 63, 73
poverty of, 24
separate schools for, 36
territorial autonomy in, 19
traditional crafts of, 47
traditional local governance mechanisms, 27, 51, 54b
mobility in, 8, 9
Pentacostals in, 52
Lesotho, 54n1
Lévi-Strauss, Claude, 28
local governments and cultural diversity, 1, 4–5, 31–55
conclusions regarding, 75–77
cultural services, 5, 46–49
designing and implementing, 5
education, 5, 31–39, 32b, 34b, 36b, 38b, 63, 76
health care, 5, 40–46, 42b, 45b, 72
by local governments, 5
national public policy, clashes with, 53, 54b
policies supporting, 5. See also policies supporting cultural diversity in service delivery
political will, existence or lack of, 66
traditional local governance systems, using, 49–54, 51b, 54b
London School of Hygiene and Tropical Medicine, 40
Loury, Glenn C., 21, 29n4

M

Madagascar, 50, 54n1
Malaysia, 8, 14, 19, 23b, 43, 73
Mali, 8, 43
Maori population of New Zealand
changes to public policy regarding, 14, 25
education, 34b, 35, 36, 37, 38, 39, 63
evaluation, need for, 73
health care, 42
inspiration for other programs drawn from, 57

integrated and multisectoral approach, 62–63
ministry for, 65
political representation for, 63, 67
marginalization of cultural groups, 69
Masai, 47–48
Mauritania, 29n9–10
Maya, 47, 73
Mead, George, 79
medical care in culturally diverse societies, 5, 40–46, 42*b*, 45*b*, 72
Mehotra, S., 34
"melting pot" ethos, loss of, 10–11
Mexico, 9, 24, 45*b*, 47, 52, 53, 54*b*, 62, 73
Middle East. *See* Arab world
migration. *See* mobility and cultural diversity
Minangkabau, 50
minority populations
designations and definitions for, 10*b*
dominant minorities, 23*b*
education curriculum, introduction of minority cultures in, 34–35
human rights and, 15
mobility of, 9–10
Mixe, 54*b*
mobility and cultural diversity, 2–3, 5n1
inequality, mobility due to, 9
internal migration, 8–9
international migration, 8–12
public policy affected by, 8–12
Moodley, Kogila A., 32–33
Moolaadé (film), 28n1
Morales, Lourdes, 54*b*
Morocco, 47
Mozambique, 8
multicultural citizenship, concept of, 14–17
multicultural societies. *See* cultural diversity
multiculturalist approach to social inclusion, 16–17
multisectoral integrated approach to cultural policies, 62–63
Myanmar, 19

N

nafgari (Indonesia), 50
national congress on cultural policies, Guatemala, 48
national frameworks for cultural diversity policies, establishing, 64–65

national minorities, defined, 10*b*
national public policy and cultural diversity, 4, 7–29
agency, concept of, 16, 17*b*, 25–26
conclusions regarding, 75–77
conflict reduction mechanisms, 26
cultural exclusion, reducing, 22
discrimination, combating, 20–22
importance of, 22–26
international recognition of cultural rights, 12–14, 13*b*
local governance principles clashing with, 53, 54*b*
management of cultural diversity through public policy, 18–22
mobility statistics affecting, 8–12
multicultural citizenship, concept of, 14–17
national congress on cultural policies, Guatemala, 48
political participation, encouraging, 19–20
poverty targeting, 23–25, 23*b*
risks of considering cultural diversity in making public policy, 26–28, 51*b*
subcultures, 11–12
Native Americans
Latin American. *See under* Latin America
North American, 47, 49
native language instruction, 33–34, 34*b*, 36–39, 40*b*, 68, 71*b*, 72, 73
Navajo, 47
New Zealand. *See* Maori population of New Zealand
NGOs. *See* nongovernmental organizations
Niger, 8
Nigeria, 19, 43, 54n1
nongovernmental organizations (NGOs)
cultural services, providing, 47–49, 55n5
as health mediators, 42*b*
language and education assistance, 38
as stakeholders, 67
North Africa, youth subculture in, 12. *See also* Arab world

O

Organization of American States (OAS), 64, 75
Ousmane, Sembène, 28n1

P

Pakistan, 19, 47
Pan American Health Organization, 55n4
Papua New Guinea, 19, 32b, 60, 73
Paraguay, 8
parent participation in educational initiatives, 39
Partido Revolucionario Institucional (PRI), Mexico, 52, 62
Pascacio, 54b
Peace and Reconciliation Commission, Guatemala, 65
Pentacostals in Latin America, 52
Peru, 8, 9, 24, 55n4
Philippines, 73
policies supporting cultural diversity in service delivery, 5, 57–74
    citizens' rights and cultural rights, balancing, 67–69
    conceptual framework for, 58–60
    conclusions regarding, 77
    costs of multicultural programs, 70–71, 71b, 73
    decentralization frameworks for, 19–20, 65–66
    employment policies, 63, 69, 70b
    evaluation processes for, 72–74
    integrated and multisectoral approach to, 62–63
    long-term nature of, 71–72
    national frameworks, establishing, 64–65
    national public policy. See national public policy and cultural diversity
political motivations, understanding, 60–62
    socioeconomic conditions, consideration of, 69, 74n2
    stakeholder participation, importance of, 66–67
    universal solutions, lack of, 60
political decentralization, 19–20, 65–66
political motivations, understanding, 60–62
political participation, public policy encouraging, 19–20
political representation of minorities, 63, 67
polygamy, 27, 28
Portillo Cabrera, Alfonso, 48
poverty
    multicultural education, need for, 39

poverty traps, 69
socioeconomic conditions of cultural groups, 69, 74n2
targeting, 23–25, 23b
preschool education, 37, 38b
PRI (Partido Revolucionario Institucional), Mexico, 52, 62
private sector involvement in commercial cultural initiatives, 49
public policy. See national public policy and cultural diversity

R

Recondo, David, 52
religion
    accommodations for, 3
    community isolation of, 69
    corporate devolution and, 20
    cultural diversity, as aspect of, 1, 7, 10, 64
    cultural exclusion, reducing, 22
    cultural minorities, defined, 10b
    cultural rights associated with, 12, 13b, 18, 20
    cultural services related to, 5, 46, 47, 50
    discrimination based on, 24
    freedom of, 18, 22, 28n2
    isolated groups, 69
    Middle East, Islamist groups of, 52
    Pentacostals in Latin America, 52
    traditional local governance forms and, 27, 31, 51, 52, 53
Republic of Korea, 14
República Bolivariana de Venezuela, 8, 19
rights, cultural. See cultural rights
Roma
    cultural centers for, 48
    education for, 36b, 38, 73
    health care for, 42–43, 42b
    labor force, participation in, 70b
    poverty targeting, 23
Romania, 23b, 42, 54, 56b, 64, 67, 73
rural-to-rural and rural-to-urban migration, 8–9

S

safety nets, economic, 69
Sartre, Jean Paul, 79
segregated schools for minorities, 36–37, 36b

self-confirming stereotypes, 29n4
self-identification, changing models of, 3–4
Sen, Amartya, 17*b*
Senegal, 9, 28n1
service delivery and cultural diversity. *See*
    cultural diversity
sistema de cargo (Latin America), 51
Slovak Republic, 36
Smith, Alana, 32
social cohesion, integration, and inclusion,
    defined, 2*b*
socioeconomic conditions of cultural
    groups, 69, 74n2
Soeharto, 50
Somalia, 54n1
South Africa, 8, 23*b*, 29n9, 73
Soviet Union, 9, 15, 40*b*
Spain, 15, 18, 57
spatial devolution, 19
stakeholder participation, importance of,
    66–67
stereotyping, 21, 29n4, 70*b*
stigma, 21
sub-Saharan Africa. *See* Africa
subcultures, 11–12
sustainable livelihoods, 47–48
Switzerland, 15, 18, 55*n*5

T

Taiwanese indigenous music, 47
Tanzania, 54n1
Taylor, Charles, 25
Thailand, 73
Tibet, 10
tontines, 26, 29n8
Totontepec, Mexico, local governance
    principles in, 53, 54*b*
Touraine, Alain, 3
tourism, cultural, 46–49
traditional arts and crafts, 47, 49
traditional local governance systems,
    delivering services through, 49–54,
    51*b*, 54*b*
traditional medicine, 43–46, 45*b*, 72
Traditions for Tomorrow, 55n5
tribal and indigenous peoples. *See* indig-
    enous peoples
Turkey, minorities within, 61
Turkish minorities of Eastern and Central
    Europe, 39

U

Uganda, 19, 54n1, 73
United Nations (UN), 12–14, 13*b*, 15, 64,
    75
United Nations Development Programme
    (UNDP), 1, 13–14, 18, 20
United Nations Educational, Scientific and
    Cultural Organization (UNESCO),
    12–13, 13*b*
United States
    African Americans in, 18, 21
    Amish in, 69
    cultural competence, concept of, 40
    integrationist approach to social inclu-
        sion in, 16
    Irish immigration to, 11
    "melting pot" ethos in, 11
Universal Declaration of Human Rights,
    12, 15
Universal Declaration on Cultural Diver-
    sity, 12–13
universal solutions, lack of, 60
urban-to-rural and urban-to-urban migra-
    tion, 9

V

Venezuela, República Bolivariana de, 8, 19
Vietnam, 24, 43, 73

W

WHO (World Health Organization),
    43–45, 55n4, 72
Wieviorka, Michel, 15
women. *See* gender issues
World Decade for Cultural Development,
    13*b*
World Health Organization (WHO),
    43–45, 55n4, 72

X

Xola (film), 28n1

Y

Young, Crawford, 60
youth
    in age-biased cultures, 27
    avoiding exclusion of, 76
    cultural identity, formation of, 80–81

stakeholder participation, importance
    of, 67
subcultures, 11–12
traditional local governance mechanisms
    and, 51–52, 51b

Yugoslavia, former, 60

Z

Zambia, 43

ECO-AUDIT
Environmental Benefits Statement

The World Bank is committed to preserving endangered forests and natural resources. The Office of the Publisher has chosen to print *Delivering Services in Multicultural Societies* on recycled paper with 30 percent postconsumer fiber in accordance with the recommended standards for paper usage set by the Green Press Initiative, a nonprofit program supporting publishers in using fiber that is not sourced from endangered forests. For more information, visit www.greenpressinitiative.org.

Saved:
- 6 trees
- 1 million British thermal units of total energy
- 247 pounds of net greenhouse gases (CO_2 equivalent)
- 1,191 gallons of waste water
- 72 pounds of solid waste

green
press
INITIATIVE